Editors

Kim Fields

Sara Connolly

Managing Editor

Ina Massler Levin, M.A.

Illustrator

Vicki Frazier

Cover Artist

Brenda DiAntonis

Art Production Manager

Kevin Barnes

Imaging

Craig Gunnell

Art Coordinator

Renée Christine Yates

Publisher

Mary D. Smith, M.S. Ed.

MASTERING SECOND GRADE SKILLS

Includes Standards & Benchmarks

Author

Susan Mackey Collins, M.Ed.

Teacher Created Resources, Inc.

6421 Industry Way

Westminster, CA 92683

www.teachercreated.com

ISBN: 978-1-4206-3957-5

©2006 Teacher Created Resources, Inc.

Reprinted, 2009

Made in U.S.A.

Table of Contents

Introduction 4

Meeting Standards 5

Grammar

Writing Sentences 7

Subjects 16

Predicates 18

Subjects and Predicates 20

Nouns 22

Pronouns 31

Adjectives 34

Verbs 37

Apostrophes 44

Commas 48

Abbreviations 55

Quotation Marks 56

Titles 58

Reading

Context Clues 59

Sequencing 62

Cause and Effect 67

Fact and Opinion 69

Compare and Contrast 71

Drawing Conclusions 74

Real or Fantasy 76

Predicting 78

Paragraphs 80

Alphabetical Order 83

Word Endings 84

Compound Words 85

Table of Contents *(cont.)*

Math

Addition. 86

Subtraction 96

Addition and Subtraction 98

Number Line. 100

Counting by Two's, Three's, Five's, and Ten's. 101

Even and Odd Numbers. 109

Estimating. 110

Comparing 112

Ordinals 115

Money. 118

Time 122

Organizing Numbers 130

Shapes 132

Measurement 137

Place Value. 145

Multiplication 151

Social Studies

Citizenship 160

Community 167

Geography 174

History 179

Maps and Graphs. 185

Science

Plants and Animals. 191

Weather 204

Earth and the Universe 210

Physical Science 216

Forces and Machines 218

Answer Key

Answer Key 222

Introduction

The wealth of knowledge a person gains throughout his or her lifetime is impossible to measure, and it will certainly vary from person to person. However, regardless of the scope of knowledge, the foundation for all learning remains a constant. All that we know and think throughout our lifetimes is based upon fundamentals, and these fundamentals are the basic skills upon which all learning develops. *Mastering Second Grade Skills* is a book that reinforces a variety of basic skills.

* **Grammar**   * **Social Studies**

* **Reading**   * **Science**

* **Math**

This book was written with the wide range of skills and ability levels of second grade students in mind. Both teachers and parents can benefit from the variety of pages provided in this book. A parent can use the book to work with his or her child to provide an introduction to new material or reinforce material already familiar to the child. Similarly, a teacher can select pages that provide additional practice for concepts taught in the classroom. When tied to what is being covered in class, pages from this book make great homework reinforcement. The worksheets provided in this book are ideal for use at home, as well as in the classroom. Research shows us that skill mastery comes with exposure and repetition. To be internalized, concepts must be reviewed until they become second nature. Parents may certainly foster the classroom experience by exposing their children to the necessary skills whenever possible, and teachers will find that these pages perfectly complement their classroom needs. An answer key, beginning on page 222, provides teachers, parents, and children with a quick method of checking responses to completed worksheets.

Basic skills are utilized every day in untold ways. Make the practice of them part of your children's or students' routines. Such work done now will benefit children in countless ways throughout their lives.

Meeting Standards

Each lesson in Mastering Second Grade Skills meets one or more of the following standards, which are used with permission from McREL (Copyright 2000 McRel, Mid-continent Research for Education and Learning. Telephone: 303-337-0990. Website: www.mcrel.org.)

Language Arts Standards	Page Number
Uses grammatical and mechanical conventions in written compositions	
* Uses complete sentences in written compositions	7–9, 13
* Uses declarative and interrogative sentences in written compositions	10
* Uses conventions of spelling in written compositions	84–85
* Uses conventions of capitalization in written compositions	24–26, 58
* Uses conventions of punctuation in written compositions	11–12, 44–58
* Uses nouns in written compositions	16–17, 20–21, 31–33
* Uses verbs in written compositions	14–15, 18–21, 37–43
* Uses adjectives in written compositions	32–34
Uses the general skills and strategies of the reading process	
* Understands how print is organized and read	83
* Uses meaning clues to aid comprehension and make predictions about content	59–61, 67–68, 78–79
Uses reading skills and strategies to understand and interpret a variety of literary texts	
* Uses reading skills and strategies to understand and interpret a variety of literary texts	69–73, 76–77
* Makes simple inferences regarding the order of events and possible outcomes	62–66, 74–75, 82
* Knows the main ideas or theme of a story	80–81

Mathematics Standards	Page Number
Uses a variety of strategies in the problem-solving process	
* Counts whole numbers	101–109, 115–117
* Understands symbolic, concrete, and pictorial representations of numbers	117, 130
Uses basic and advanced procedures while performing the process of computation	
* Adds and subtracts whole numbers	86–99
* Solves real-world problems involving addition and subtraction of whole numbers	127
* Understands basic estimation strategies and terms	110–113, 137
* Makes quantitative estimates of familiar linear dimensions, weights, and time intervals and checks them against measurements	137
* Understands the inverse relationship between addition and subtraction	98
* Understands the basic measures length, width, height, weight, and temperature	137, 143–144
* Understands the concept of time and how it is measured	122–128
* Knows process for telling time, counting money, and measuring length, weight, and temperature, using basic standards and non-standard units	118–121, 138–141
* Understands basic properties of and similarities and differences between simple geometric shapes	136
* Understands the common language of spatial sense	114, 146, 149–150
* Understands that observations about objects or events can be organized and displayed in simple graphs	131
* Recognizes regularities in a variety of contexts	132–135, 145,
* Uses basic and advanced procedures while performing the processes of computation	147–148, 151–160

Meeting Standards (cont.)

Social Studies Standards	Page Number
Understands and knows how to analyze chronological relationships and patterns	
* Understands and knows how to analyze chronological relationshipsand patterns	181–182
* Understands family life now and in the past, and family life in various places long ago	179–180
Understands how individuals have worked to achieve the liberties and equalities promised in the principles of American democracy and to improve the lives of people from many groups	
* Understands how democratic values came to be, and how they have been exemplified by people, events, and symbols	160, 162, 164–166
* Knows how different groups of people in the community have taken responsibility for the common good	160, 167–169, 171–173
* Knows the history of American symbols	162, 166
* Understands the causes and nature of movements of large groups of people into and within the United States, now and long ago	183
* Understands the reasons that Americans celebrate certain national holidays	184
* Knows the location of places, geographic features, and patterns of the environment	170, 173, 186, 188–190
* Understands the physical and human characteristics of place	173–174, 187
* Understands the characteristics and uses of maps, globes, and other geographic tools and technologies	177–178

Science Standards	Page Number
Understands atmospheric processes and the water cycle	
* Knows that short-term weather conditions and weather patterns change over the seasons	204–206, 208–209
* Understands atmospheric processes and the water cycle	207
Understands the composition and structure of the universe and Earth's place in it	
* Understands the composition and structure of the universe and Earth's place in it	212–215
Understands the principles of heredity and related concepts	
* Knows that plants and animals closely resemble their parents	201
Understands the structure and function of cells and organisms	
* Knows the basic needs of plants and animals	191–192
* Knows that plants and animals have features that help them live in different environments	197–199
Understands relationships among organisms and their physical environment	
* Understands relationships among organisms and their physical environment	193–196, 200, 203
Understands biological evolution and the diversity of life	
* Understands biological evolution and the diversity of life	202, 210–211
Understands the structure and properties of matter	
* Understands the structure and properties of matter	216–217
Understands forces and motion	
* Knows that position and motion of an object can be changed by pushing or pulling	218–219
* Understands forces and motion	220–221

It's a Sentence!

A sentence makes a complete thought. A sentence also begins with a capital letter and ends with a period (.), a question mark (?), or an exclamation point (!).

Example: Birthdays are a lot of fun.

Rewrite the sentences below. Be sure to begin each one with a capital letter. Add correct ending punctuation to each sentence.

1. is today your birthday

Is today your birthday?

2. a party is a wonderful idea

A party is wonderful idea.

3. mike will bring the birthday cake

4. how many candles will be on the cake

5. will there be a clown

6. we can help you decorate

7. karen will bring the balloons

8. the party will have lots of music

9. there will be many presents

10. what a wonderful birthday it will be

I'll Have My Sentence with Ketchup, Please

A sentence must include a complete thought. The words you read must make sense. Words grouped together that do not make a complete thought do not make a sentence.

> French fries are delicious. (sentence)
> Ketchup on my fries. (not a sentence)

Look at the group of words written on each french fry below.

If the group of words is a sentence, color it red.

If the group of words is not a sentence, color it yellow.

1. Chocolate shakes and malts.
2. A double cheeseburger is great.
3. How many french fries can you eat?
4. One potato.
5. Baked potatoes are yummy, too!
6. Green ketchup is.
7. Fries are a special treat to eat.
8. You need to use a napkin.
9. Do you like hamburgers?
10. Crispy fries are the best.

French Fries

Picture This Sentence

Look at each picture. Then write a complete sentence explaining each picture.
Remember to use a capital letter to start each sentence. Be sure to end each
sentence with an end mark.

1.

_____

2.

_____

3.

_____

4.

_____

On the back of this page, draw a picture of the sentence below.

I saw a rainbow in the sky.

Alike and Different

Each sentence has two things: it starts with a capital letter and ends with an end mark. But, all end marks are not the same.

A sentence that is a statement ends with a period (.).

I love green beans.

A sentence that is a question ends with a question mark (?).

Do you love green beans?

For each question, write a statement. For each statement, write a question.

1. What is your name?

_____

2. How old are you?

_____

3. What is your favorite color?

_____

4. Do you have a pet?

_____

5. My teacher reads to us.

_____

6. Today is a school day.

_____

More Alike and Different

You know a sentence begins with a capital letter and has an end mark at the end, but did you know there are different kinds of sentences?

A command sentence ends with a period (.). A command sentence tells someone what to do.

Throw litter in the trash.

An exclamation sentence shows strong emotion and ends with an exclamation point (!).

Today is my birthday!

Read each sentence. Put a period at the end if the sentence is a command. Put an exclamation point at the end if the sentence is an exclamation.

1. Go to the office

2. I've got to see the principal

3. I'm in big trouble

4. Shut the door

5. Tell me what you did

6. I can't believe you put gum on the teacher's chair

7. Bring your books and come with me

8. Tell the teacher you are sorry

Just for fun: On the back of this paper, draw a picture showing how happy you are to be at school!

Know Your End Marks

A sentence begins with a capital letter, but don't forget how a sentence ends. Each sentence must have an end mark.

A statement ends with a period (.). A question ends with a question mark (?). A command ends with a period (.). An exclamation ends with an exclamation point (!).

Read each sentence. Write a C if the sentence is correct. If the sentence is not correct, cross out the incorrect end mark and write the correct end mark.

_____ **1.** I like playing in the snow?

_____ **2.** Have you ever built a snowman?

_____ **3.** Hey, watch out for that slippery ice!

_____ **4.** I wish it would snow a little each day.

_____ **5.** Hot chocolate tastes good on a cold day!

_____ **6.** Do you want to ride my sled.

_____ **7.** The snow will melt when the sun comes out!

_____ **8.** How beautiful the snow is.

_____ **9.** I wear my mittens when it is cold.

_____ **10.** Do you think winter is the best season?

Complete and Incomplete

A sentence tells a complete thought. An incomplete sentence does not tell a complete thought.

     My dog has fleas. (sentence)

     My dog. (incomplete sentence)

This group of words does not have a predicate. It does not make a complete thought.

Read each group of words. Use a yellow crayon to circle each complete sentence. Help Rover find his way home and avoid the mean cats along the way.

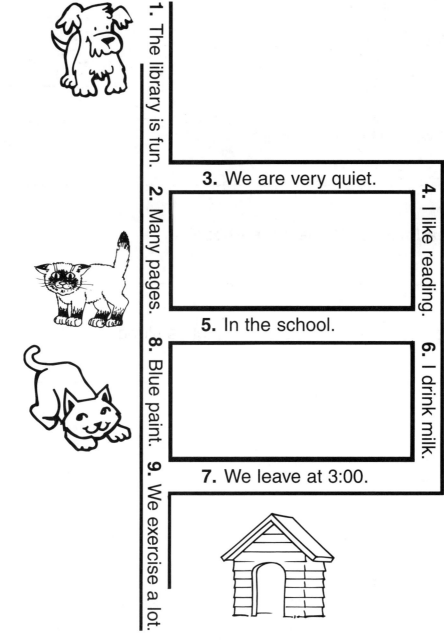

1. The library is fun.

2. Many pages.

3. We are very quiet.

4. I like reading.

5. In the school.

6. I drink milk.

7. We leave at 3:00.

8. Blue paint.

9. We exercise a lot.

Make Mine a Combo

Some things go together like a hamburger and fries or peanut butter and jelly. Some sentences go together, too.

To combine two sentences, check to see if the sentences have the same predicate. Sentences that have the same predicate can be joined together with the word *and*.

> Brett ran the race. Sadie ran the race.
> Brett **and** Sadie ran the race.

Read the sentences. Use the word *and* to help you combine the sentences to create a new sentence.

1. Cows eat hay. Horses eat hay.

_____

2. The ducks swim. The geese swim.

_____

3. Teachers read books. Students read books.

_____

4. Some of the pigs sleep. Some of the piglets sleep.

_____

5. Sheep graze. Goats graze.

_____

More of the Same

Sometimes the subjects of two sentences are the same, but the predicates are different.

Two sentences with the same subject can be joined by using the word *and*.

David kicked the ball. David ran to first base.
David kicked the ball **and** ran to first base.

Read the following sentence pairs. Write a new sentence using the word *and*.

1. My family laughs at jokes.
My family cries at sad movies.

_____

2. The doctor met us at the hospital.
The doctor told us where to wait.

_____

3. Kayla caught a bug.
Kayla kept a bug.

_____

4. The team won the game.
The team was given a trophy.

_____

5. We ate sandwiches.
We ate carrots.

_____

Who or What Is It All About?

The subject of the sentence tells who or what does something.

In the nursery rhyme, "Jack Be Nimble," Jack was quick when he jumped over the candle stick. Jack is the subject.

Jack was quick.

Jack jumped over the candle stick.

Look at each picture clue below and then write the subject for each sentence.

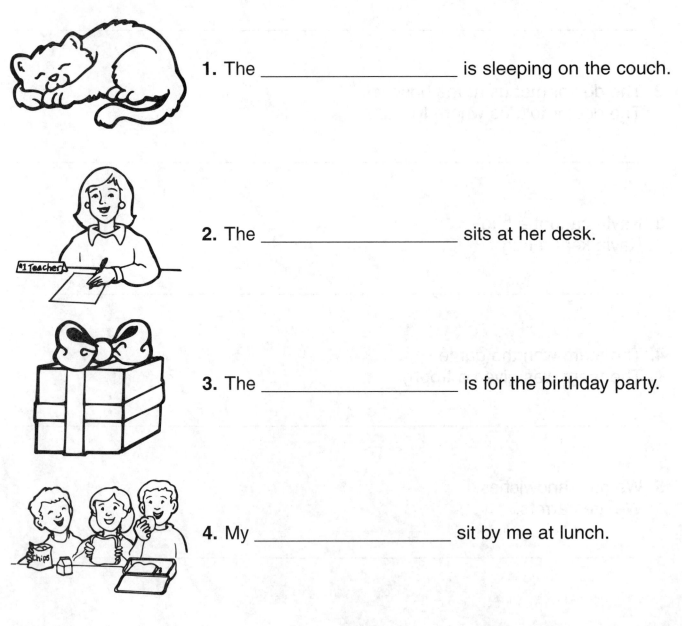

1. The _____ is sleeping on the couch.

2. The _____ sits at her desk.

3. The _____ is for the birthday party.

4. My _____ sit by me at lunch.

Find That Subject!

Don't forget: The subject of the sentence tells who or what the sentence is about.

Circle the subject in each sentence.

1. Many students visit the zoo each year.

2. The zoo is fun to visit.

3. Many different animals are found at the zoo.

4. The monkeys swing from tree to tree.

5. The elephants play in the water.

6. One elephant sprays water on us.

7. A man shows us a baby bird.

8. The giraffe is my favorite animal to visit.

9. We will visit the zoo again.

Now write your own sentence about the zoo. Circle the subject.

10.

_____

_____

Make a Splash with Predicates

Look at the picture below. Then write a predicate in each sentence. Use the words in the box to help you.

is	wears	standing	slides	splash

1. One girl is _____ by the water.

2. The pool _____ a fun place to play.

3. Do not _____ water on the towels!

4. Mary is safe at the pool when she _____ her lifejacket.

5. Jack _____ down the big slide into the water.

Now write a sentence of your own about a day at the pool. Circle each predicate.

_____

_____

More Fun with Predicates

Look at the raindrops below. If a raindrop has a predicate, color it blue.

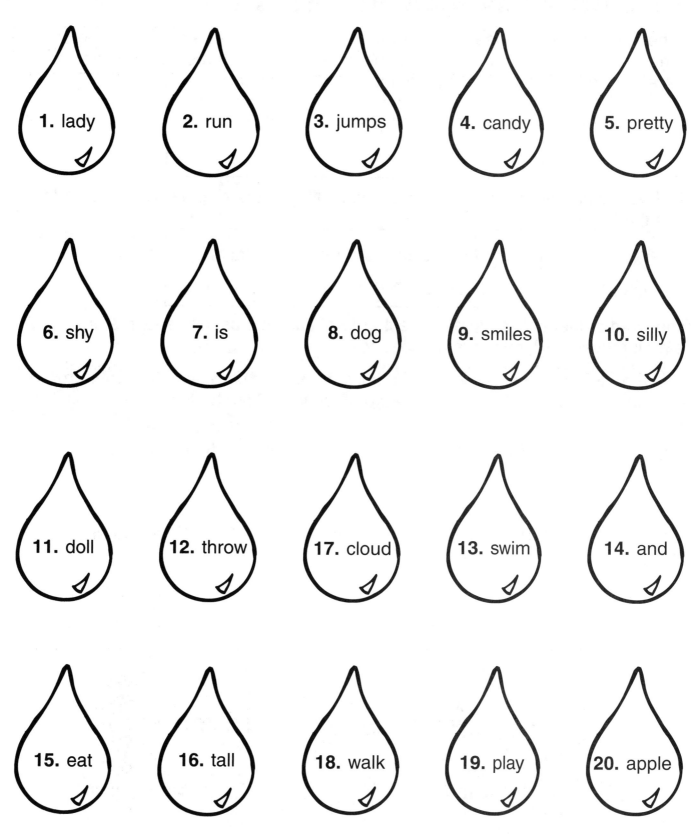

1. lady

2. run

3. jumps

4. candy

5. pretty

6. shy

7. is

8. dog

9. smiles

10. silly

11. doll

12. throw

17. cloud

13. swim

14. and

15. eat

16. tall

18. walk

19. play

20. apple

Some Things Have to Agree

Subjects and verbs must agree or go together. The subject is who or what the sentence is about. The verb tells what the subject is doing.

If the subject is about one person or thing, the verb must be about one person or thing. Singular verbs usually end in the letter *s*. Plural verbs, or verbs about more than one person or thing, do not end in the letter *s*.

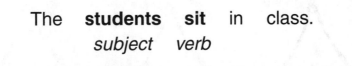

| **Andrea** | **sits** | in | class. |
| *subject* | *verb* | | |

Andrea is one person or a singular subject. Notice the singular verb *sits* ends with the letter *s*.

| The | **students** | **sit** | in | class. |
| | *subject* | *verb* | | |

The word students is a plural subject. Plural subjects usually end in *s* or *es*. *Sit* is a plural verb. Plural verbs do not end in *s*.

Read the following sentences. If the subject and verb are singular, write an *S* on the line. If the subject and verb are plural, write a *P* on the line.

_____ **1.** Millie sings.   _____ **6.** Ice melts.

_____ **2.** Brett talks.   _____ **7.** A cat meows.

_____ **3.** Students write.   _____ **8.** Dogs bark.

_____ **4.** Players win.   _____ **9.** Maids clean.

_____ **5.** Girls smile.   _____ **10.** Mary jumps.

It Must Agree

Subjects and verbs must agree. If a subject is singular, the verb must be singular. If the subject is plural, the verb must be plural.

Color only the pictures where the subject and the predicate agree.

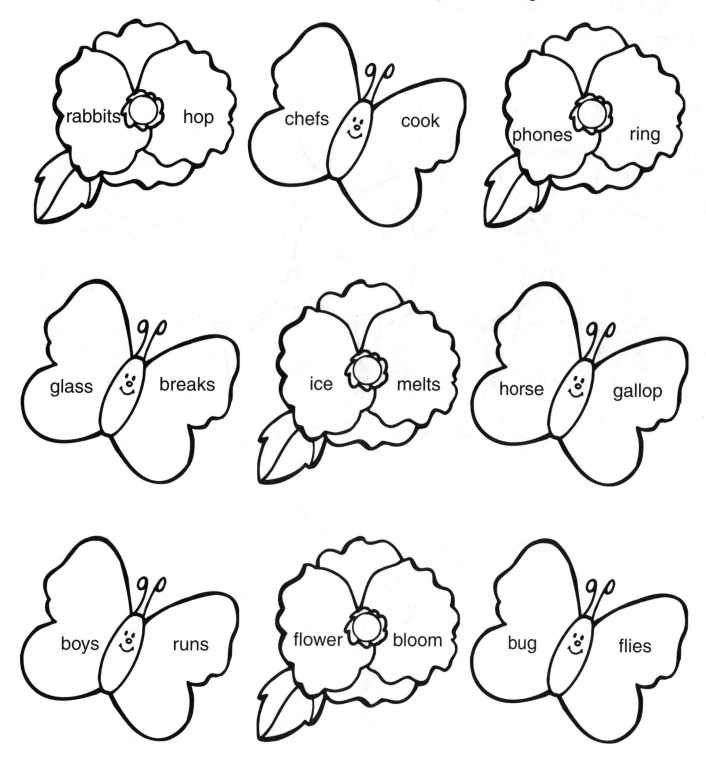

Knowing Nouns

A noun is a person, place, or thing.

Color each noun that is a person red.

Color each noun that is a place yellow.

Color each noun that is a thing blue.

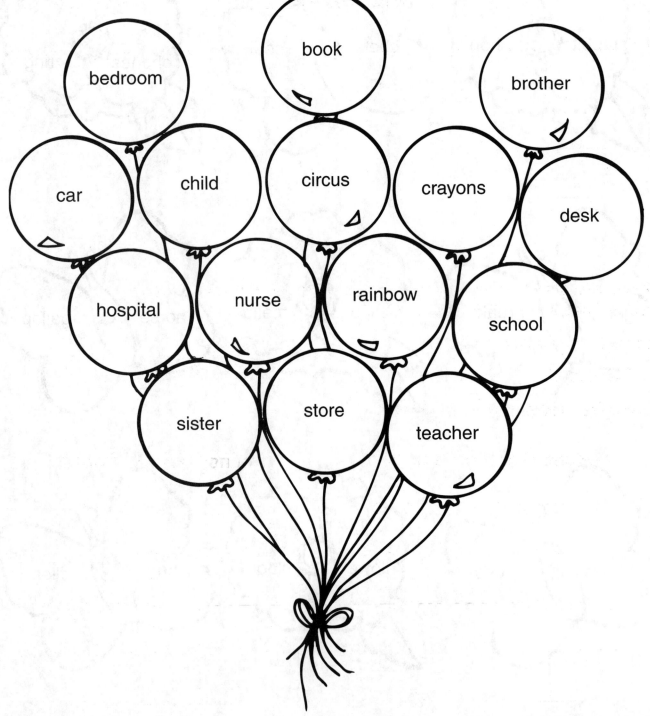

What Do You See?

A noun is a person, place, or thing. A noun is everything you see. Look around you. If you can see it, it is a noun.

Look around the room. List 10 nouns that are things.

Example: shoes

Nouns That Are Things:

1. _____   6. _____

2. _____   7. _____

3. _____   8. _____

4. _____   9. _____

5. _____   10. _____

Nouns are also places and people. List five people nouns and five place nouns.
Nouns That Are People:

Examples: teacher, Irene

Nouns That Are Places:

Examples: North America, library

Nouns That Are People: ## Nouns That Are Places:

1. _____   1. _____

2. _____   2. _____

3. _____   3. _____

4. _____   4. _____

5. _____   5. _____

It's Important to Be Proper!

Some nouns are proper nouns and need a capital letter. Proper nouns name a certain person, place, or thing.

cousin   Allison

park   River Oaks Park

dog   Princess

Look at the chart below. Some spaces are missing common nouns or nouns that aren't capitalized. Some spaces are missing proper nouns or nouns that are capitalized. Fill in each blank with the right type of noun.

		common noun	proper noun
1.		cat	
2.			Mr. Jones
3.		school	
4.			Pittsburgh
5.			Sandra
6.		cartoon	

More Proper Nouns

Proper nouns are capitalized. A proper noun names a specific person, place, or thing.

Read the sentences below. Circle each proper noun that needs a capital letter.

1. On saturday my friend and I went to the mall.

2. We went to his favorite store called more candy.

3. Mr. rapone, the owner of the store, was there.

4. My friend jack knows Mr. Rapone.

5. They both live on elm street.

6. He gave Jack and me some new candy named chocolicious.

7. It was delicious, and I told mr. Rapone thank you.

8. He told Jack to bring his sisters carole and rhonda by the store for some candy, too.

9. Jack said he would bring them by on valentine's day.

10. Mr. Rapone agreed that jack's idea was a good one.

Write a sentence about your favorite store. Be sure to use at least one proper noun.

_____

_____

Your Favorite Proper Nouns

Don't forget: A proper noun names a certain person, place, or thing and is always capitalized.

Fill in each blank with your favorite proper noun. Remember to capitalize your answers.

My Personal Favorites

1. My favorite movie is ___X Games_____.

2. My favorite place to eat out is ___chilies_____.

3. My favorite game is ___halo_____.

4. My favorite snack food is ___Steak_____.

5. Some of my favorite people are ___Joeseph_____.

6. My favorite holiday is ___christmas_____.

7. My favorite month is ___April_____.

8. My favorite day of the week is ___Friday_____.

9. My favorite book is ___The Great White_____.

10. My favorite song is _____.

Singular and Plural

Some nouns are singular and some nouns are plural. A singular noun names one person, place, or thing. A plural noun names more than one person, place, or thing.

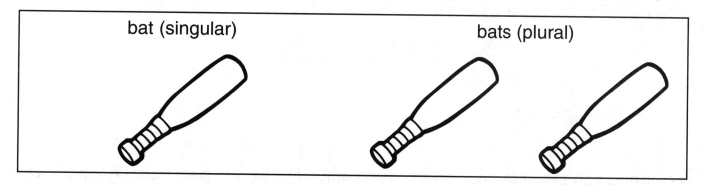

bat (singular)   bats (plural)

Look at the list of nouns. Write S beside the noun if it is singular. Write P beside the noun if it is plural.

_____ **1.** boxes

_____ **2.** children

_____ **3.** cow

_____ **4.** students

_____ **5.** trees

_____ **6.** mice

_____ **7.** glasses

_____ **8.** fork

_____ **9.** marbles

_____ **10.** phone

_____ **11.** ball

_____ **12.** worms

_____ **13.** feathers

_____ **14.** egg

_____ **15.** geese

_____ **16.** lunch

_____ **17.** friend

_____ **18.** cars

_____ **19.** son

_____ **20.** girls

Magical Plurals

Changing a singular noun to a plural noun is like doing a magic trick. With a wave of your magical wand (otherwise known as your pencil), you can change singular nouns to plural nouns quicker than you can pull a rabbit out of a hat! All you need to know are a few simple tricks:

Add an *s* to change most singular nouns to a plural noun.

camel   camels

Add an *es* to change singular nouns that end with *s, x, sh,* or *ch.*

fox   foxes

Change each singular noun to a plural noun. Write each new plural noun inside the hat.

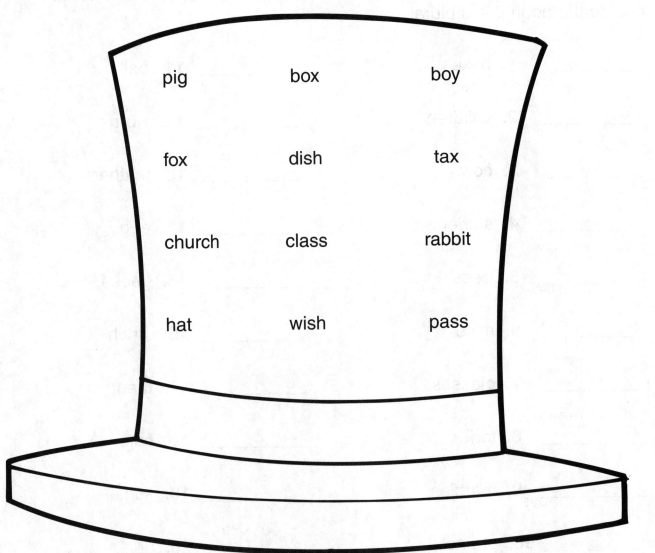

pig   box   boy

fox   dish   tax

church   class   rabbit

hat   wish   pass

More Rules for Plurals

If you want to make a plural with words ending in a consonant and a *y*, you must change the *y* to the letter *i* and then add *es*.

berry   berries

Some plural nouns follow other rules. These tricky nouns change their entire spelling to become plural!

ox becomes oxen   goose becomes geese   man becomes men

Look at each set of words and circle the word that has used the plural rule correctly.

1. a. ladys

b. ladies

2. a. mouses

b. mice

3. a. babies

b. babys

4. a. foots

b. feet

5. a. puppys

b. puppies

6. a. jellys

b. jellies

7. a. women

b. womans

8. a. children

b. childrens

9. a. teeth

b. tooths

10. a. gooses

b. geese

Picture These Plurals

Add the correct ending to change each singular noun to a plural noun. Write the new noun on the line provided.

1. bird _____

6. daddy _____

2. family _____

7. glass _____

3. porch _____

8. fox _____

4. dinosaur _____

9. city _____

5. mother _____

10. hanger _____

Almost a Noun

A pronoun takes the place of a noun.

Riley   is a dancer.   She   is graceful.

(noun)   (pronoun)

Fill in the blank with the correct pronoun.

1. My dad loves apples, and _____ do too.

2. _____ eat them every day.

3. Apples are a fruit, and _____ keep you healthy.

4. My sister likes apples, but _____ can't eat them right now.

5. She is missing _____ two front teeth!

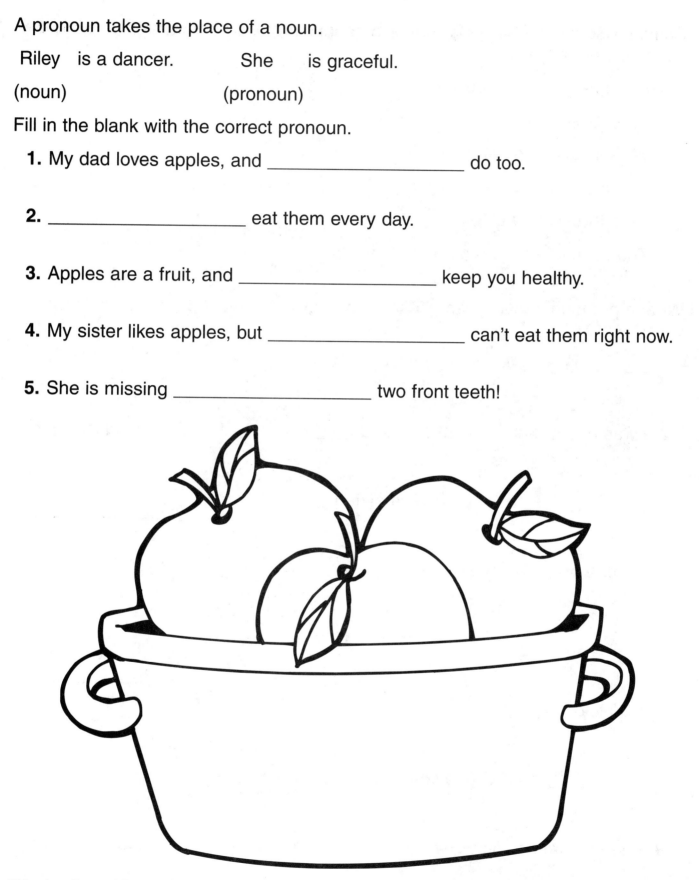

Using Pronouns

Some pronouns are subjects. Other pronouns are used after action verbs and can never be subjects.

I and *we* are subject pronouns.

    I play baseball.

    We will have a great team.

Me and *us* are not subject pronouns. They are used after the verb.

    Jana threw me the ball.

    The coach gave us a party.

Write a pronoun in each blank. If the pronoun is a subject pronoun, circle the word.

1. _____ like to go camping.

2. I was happy when my father asked _____ to go camping last week.

3. _____ camped in a small tent.

4. No one else went with _____ .

5. _____ sat around the campfire.

6. Dad told _____ some scary stories.

7. _____ told Dad some stories, too.

8. I hope Mom can go with _____ next time.

Those Possessive Pronouns

Possessive pronouns show ownership. Possessive pronouns do not use apostrophes to show ownership.

    Correct: That is his horse.

    Incorrect: That is his's horse.

Circle the correct possessive pronoun.

1. My cousin has his/his's own horse.

2. Its/Its' name is Star.

3. Her/Her's fur is soft like a rabbit.

4. I think my/my's cousin is so lucky.

5. I wish I had a horse that was all mine/mine's.

Write a possessive pronoun in each blank. You can use a word more than once. Use the words in the box.

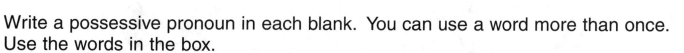

my	her	your	his

6. _____ teacher is very nice.

7. If you are good, _____ desk will have a surprise on it each morning.

8. _____ name is Mrs. Mackey.

9. _____ class gets to have recess every day.

10. My friend Tristan brought _____ basketball to recess.

Describe Those Words!

An adjective describes a noun.

My friend is pretty.

In this sentence, *pretty* is the adjective.

My little sister has straight teeth.

In this sentence, *little* and *straight* are adjectives.

Look at each picture. On the line provided, write two adjectives to describe each picture.

Some Adjectives Are Special

The words *a, an,* and *the* are adjectives. They are used so much in writing that they also have a special name. They are called articles.

The words *a* and *an* also have a special job.

Use *a* in front of words that start with a consonant.

    a clock

    a telephone

Use *an* in front of words that start with a vowel or vowel sound.

    an apple

    an adjective

The word *the* can be used in front of words that start with a vowel or a consonant.

    the apple

    the computer

Read each sentence. Circle the correct answer.

1. A/An orange tastes better than an apple.

2. We went to a/an movie Friday night.

3. My mother bought a/an magazine to read.

4. Here are the/a tickets.

5. Can you get me the/an remote?

6. That is a/an beautiful lady.

7. A/An alligator lives in warm water.

8. The/An teacher is talking.

9. Why does a/an ogre scare people?

10. A/An rainbow is many different colors.

Adjectives Do More Than Describe

Adjectives can be used to compare nouns. To compare two nouns, add *er* to the end of most adjectives.

Kelly is older than her sister.

Add *est* to the end of most adjectives to compare more than two nouns.

Kelly is the youngest of all her sisters.

Complete each sentence by adding an adjective of your own.

1. My house is the _____ one on the street.

2. Kara's cat is _____ than your cat.

3. English class is _____ than math class.

4. Is my hair _____ than yours?

5. Popcorn with butter is _____ than popcorn without butter.

6. Summer is usually _____ than spring.

7. A watermelon is the _____ fruit.

8. You are the _____ boy I know.

9. Loretta is _____ than Robert.

10. This is the _____ day ever.

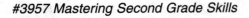

Verbs Have Action!

An action verb shows the action in a sentence.

Janie swims in the pool.

Karen dives in the water.

Shelby jumps off the diving board.

Color all of the action verbs below yellow. When you are done, you will be able to finish this secret code: "_____ is for verb."

jump	kitty	cup	vase	eat
napkin	smile	doll	stand	computer
water	mouse	sit	ruler	scissors

Go, Verb, Go!

An action verb shows the action in a sentence. The action verb shows what someone or something is doing.

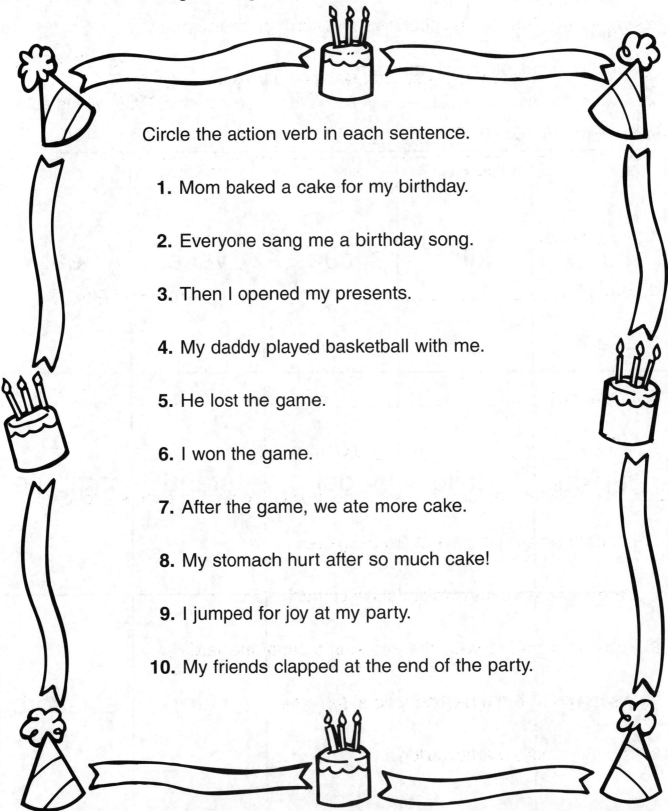

Circle the action verb in each sentence.

1. Mom baked a cake for my birthday.

2. Everyone sang me a birthday song.

3. Then I opened my presents.

4. My daddy played basketball with me.

5. He lost the game.

6. I won the game.

7. After the game, we ate more cake.

8. My stomach hurt after so much cake!

9. I jumped for joy at my party.

10. My friends clapped at the end of the party.

When Did It Happen?

Verbs have tense. This means a verb tells when the action takes place. Did the action happen in the past? Is the action happening in the present?

Present tense: She makes cookies. She watches television.

Past tense: She made cookies. She watched television.

Look at the words in the box. Add a present tense verb to each sentence.

sits	crawls	eats	meets	walks

1. My little sister _____ across the floor.

2. Mrs. Willis _____ more pizza than anyone I know.

3. Braden _____ quietly in church.

4. My mother _____ all my new friends.

5. Natalie _____ five miles every day.

Read the following sentences. Circle the past tense verb in each sentence.

6. I eat/ate seven hot dogs at the ballgame.

7. Caroline wins/won the talent show contest.

8. Bob and James dig/dug the tree stump out of the yard.

9. Tessa and Karen shop/shopped at the mall.

10. The play finally starts/started.

Special Verbs

Verbs can be in the present tense or the past tense. Many verbs add the letters *ed* to make the past tense of the verb.

skip   skipped

(present)   (past)

But some verbs are special. These special verbs do not add the letters *ed* to the end of the past tense verb. Instead they form the past tense of the verb in different ways.

Look at the word *go*. The word *go* in the past tense becomes *went*.

Present tense: I go to the store.

Past tense: I went to the store.

Match each present tense verb to its correct past tense.

1. do   **a.** sang

2. say   **b.** did

3. see   **c.** saw

4. run   **d.** said

5. come   **e.** gave

6. give   **f.** ran

7. sing   **g.** came

8. have   **h.** had

Write two sentences about something you did yesterday.

Be sure to use past tense verbs. Circle each verb.

9. _____

10. _____

Helping Out

Some words need help. Action verbs often need help to show the action in a sentence. Helping verbs help show the action.

Bo	is	swimming	in the pool.
	helping verb	action verb	

There are many helping verbs, but here are a few of them:

is, are, was, were, has, and *have.*

Add a helping verb to each sentence. You can use the same helping verb more than once.

1. She _____ cooking her pizza.

2. Kenneth _____ made his project.

3. Aunt Marie and I _____ going to the mall.

4. We _____ planned your party.

5. They _____ making a mess.

Look at the picture below. Write a sentence about what is happening in the picture. Be sure to use a helping verb.

_____

Linking It Together

A linking verb links the subject to another word.

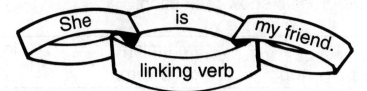

The word *is* links the word *she* to the word *friend*.

There are many linking verbs, but here are some of them:

is, are, was, were, am.

Read each sentence. Cut out each word. Link each subject to another word by placing a linking verb in the middle. Tape the linking verb to two other words to create a sentence.

She	is	funny.
They	are	moving.
Kara	is	pretty.
Derek	is	eating.
Frogs	are	green.

Which One's Which?

Action verbs show what the subject is doing. Linking verbs link the subject to another word. Can you tell which verbs show action and which verbs are linking?

Read the paragraph.

Circle the action verbs.

Cross out the linking verbs.

I wanted a pet. For my birthday my mother bought me a hamster. My hamster is brown. I named him T. Rex. He is tall for a hamster. He also bit everyone in my family. I love him anyway. He is a good pet. T. Rex just needs a little training. I like him very much.

Whose Is It?

A possessive noun shows possession or ownership. Adding an apostrophe (')
and the letter *s* to a singular noun shows that something belongs to the noun.

This is Jack.

This is Jack's puppy.

This is a puppy.

Use the names of people you know to fill in the blanks. Don't forget to make
each singular noun possessive.

Example:

_____Terrell's_____ desk

1. _____ gold

2. _____ money

3. _____ treasure

4. _____ crown

5. _____ riches

6. _____ jewels

7. _____ trophy

8. _____ prize

9. _____ award

10. _____ surprise

Lots of Owners

A plural noun can be possessive, or own something. For a plural noun that ends in *s* or *es* to own something, just add an apostrophe (') at the end of the word.

Example: the kids' toys

Some nouns are plural but don't end in an *s* like *mice* and *men*. For these nouns to be possessive, add an apostrophe and an *s*.

Draw a line and match each plural noun to an object. Add an apostrophe or an apostrophe and the letter *s* to the word to show ownership.

1. libraries		**a.**	bottles
2. countries		**b.**	toys
3. children		**c.**	hay
4. women		**d.**	classes
5. teachers		**e.**	cities
6. cows		**f.**	cheese
7. mice		**g.**	pond
8. babies		**h.**	patients
9. doctors		**i.**	purses
10. ducks		**j.**	books

Putting Words Together

An apostrophe (') can be used to form a contraction. In a contraction, two words are shortened into one word.

does not   doesn't

cannot   can't

The apostrophe stands for the letter or letters that are left out.

Read the words by each clown, and then write the contraction of the words on the blank.

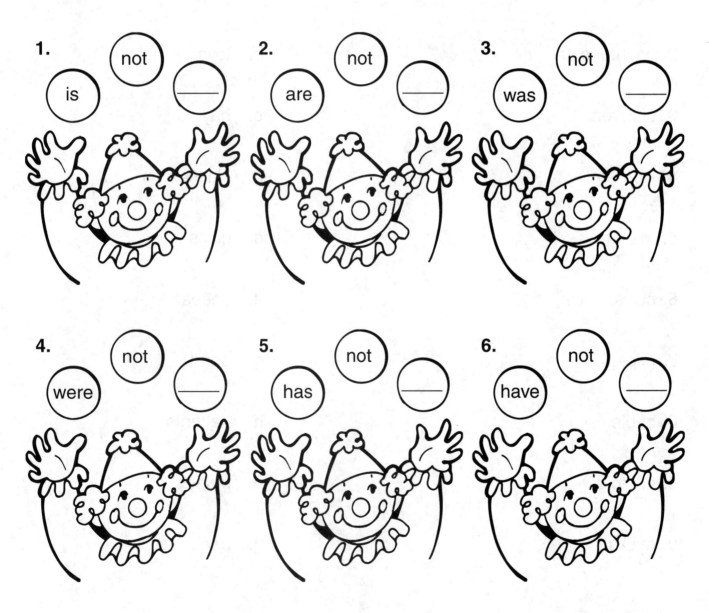

1. is not ___

2. are not ___

3. was not ___

4. were not ___

5. has not ___

6. have not ___

More Words Together

An apostrophe can be used to help form new words. Pronouns and verbs can be combined by using an apostrophe.

he	+	is	=	he's
(pronoun)		(verb)		

Read the two words in the first column. Then write the contraction on the blank in the second column.

1. she is_____

2. we are _____

3. they are _____

4. we will _____

5. it is _____

6. you are _____

7. I am_____

8. she will _____

9. they will _____

10. he would _____

Commas, Commas, and More Commas

Use commas to separate items in a series. Remember, you must have at least three items to have a group or series.

Look at each present. Look at how each gift box is shaped. Then write a list of three things that might be in the box.

Remember to use commas to separate the items in each list.

1.  _____

2.  _____

3.  _____

4.  _____

5. _____

6. _____

Caterpillar Capers

Use commas when you want to separate words in a group.

I love pizza, chocolate, and juice.

Look carefully at each caterpillar.

Read the words in each of the three circles.

Write a sentence using each list.

1.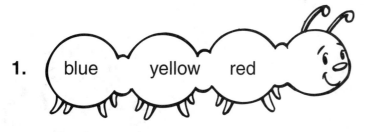
   blue   yellow   red

_____

2.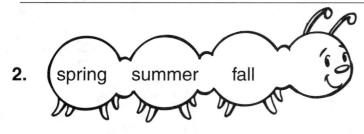
   spring   summer   fall

_____

3.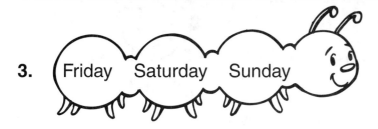
   Friday   Saturday   Sunday

_____

4.
   vanilla   chocolate strawberry

_____

5.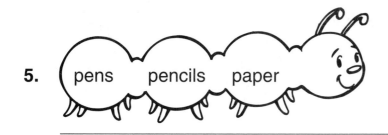
   pens   pencils   paper

_____

Know Where They Go

Remember to use commas when you want to separate items in a group or series.

Example: Allison, Kristen, and Derek cried during the part of the movie where Old Yeller died.

Read the sentences below. Add commas where they are needed.

1. January February and March are usually cold months.

2. I like ballet jazz and tap.

3. My teachers are Mrs. Winters Mr. Graves Mrs. Willis and Miss Scott.

4. He rode a train a plane and a car.

5. My favorite animals are dogs cats and rabbits.

6. Mercury Venus and Mars are all near Earth.

7. Alicia Dewanna and Olivia all forgot their money.

8. Her favorite sports are softball basketball and soccer.

9. She had a penny a nickel and a dime.

10. The girl will wash dry and curl her hair.

Separate Those Dates

Use a comma between the date and year.

I was born on February 19, 1989.

Answer each question. Use commas as needed.

1. When were you born? _____

2. Find the person sitting closest to you. When was he or she born?

_____

3. When is Valentine's Day this year? _____

4. What is the first day of the year? _____

5. What is the last day of the year? _____

6. What is today's date? _____

Add commas as needed.

7. January 6 1930   **10.** April 20 1967

8. March 3 1997   **11.** July 4 1776

9. September 12 2006   **12.** August 10 1973

AUGUST 1966						
SUN	MON	TUES	WED	THURS	FRI	SAT
	1	2	3	4	5	6
7	8	9	10	11	12	13
14	15	16	17	18	19	20
21	22	23	24	25	26	27
28	29	30	31			

Commas Rule!

When you write an address, add a comma between the city and the state.

Ann lives in Nashville, Tennessee.

Add commas as needed.

1. The plane landed in Atlanta Georgia.

2. Each spring my grandmother visits Park City Utah.

3. My pen pal lives in Decatur Alabama.

4. Movies are made in Hollywood California.

Answer the questions. Add commas as needed.

5. In what city and state do you live? _____

6. In what city and state is your school? _____

7. What is your favorite city and state? _____

8. What city and state do you most want to visit? _____

The Perfect Letter

A comma comes after the greeting or salutation of a letter.

Dear Aunt Clara,

A comma also comes after the closing of a letter.

Love always,

Betty Sue

Write a note to your teacher asking for more parties in class. Use commas after the greeting and closing.

Date _____

Dear _____

Sincerely _____

_____

More Hi's and Bye's

Friendly letters have a greeting at the beginning of the letter. They also have a closing at the end of the letter.

Always place a comma after the greeting and closing of the friendly letter.

Dear Aunt Sally,

Thank you for letting me come to your house. I had a wonderful time. It was great to eat all the crackers I wanted to eat without having to fight my parrot for them.

Love,

Janet

Rewrite each greeting or closing. Add commas as needed.

1. Dear Karen_____

2. Dear Aunt Sheryl _____

3. Dear Curt _____

4. Dear Coach Carter _____

5. Love you _____

6. Sincerely _____

7. Yours truly _____

Short and Simple

An abbreviation makes something short and simple when you have to write it. An abbreviation starts with a capital letter and is generally followed by a period; there are some exceptions such as postal abbreviations.

Instead of writing Mister Mickey you can write Mr. Mickey.

Match the following abbreviations to the correct word.

1. Dr.   **a.** mister

2. TN   **b.** street

3. Sgt.   **c.** Tennessee

4. St.   **d.** doctor

5. Mr.   **e.** junior

6. Jr.   **f.** sergeant

Add a period to each abbreviation.

7. I live at 321 Powder Mill Dr in Oak City.

8. At the hospital, I met Dr Richards.

9. Ms Rose is my teacher.

10. Mr and Mrs Boyte will attend the party.

What Was Said

Write quotation marks (" ") around what a person says.

Jack said, "How are you?"
Monica answered, "Great. I just won a million dollars!"

Below are two funny monsters, Sue and Lou. Write what you think Sue and Lou are saying. Be sure to use quotation marks.

Sue said,   Lou answered,

Now draw a picture of a new monster named Boo. Then write a sentence for Boo to say.

Boo said, _____

More Talk

Quotation marks are placed around a person's exact words.

Mr. Brinkley said, "No more monkeys jumping on the bed."

Read each sentence. Add quotation marks if needed. Write *C* if the sentence is correct.

_____**1.** Makayla said, You are very nice.

_____**2.** I enjoy reading books, Jason said.

_____**3.** Mom asked, "Are you ready for supper?"

_____**4.** Samantha said, We're going to be late.

_____**5.** The dentist asked, Do you brush your teeth?

_____**6.** The teacher said, "Do your homework, class."

_____**7.** "I don't want to take a bath!" Andy cried.

_____**8.** Courtney said, Spinach is delicious.

Terrific Titles

Underline the title of a book. Also capitalize the first and last words of a title. Capitalize any other important words in the title.

My favorite book is <u>Don't Eat My Chocolate</u> by Hungry Man.

Look at the picture on each book. Create a title for each picture book. Write the new title on the line below the book.

What Does It Mean?

Use context clues to learn new words. Context clues are words or sentences that help you figure out a new word's meaning.

My room is too messy. A messy room is never tidy. I need to clean my room more often.

If you used context clues, you were able to see that the word tidy means neat. Tidy is the opposite of messy.

Read the paragraph.

Use context clues to learn what each word means.

Fill in the circle beside the word that has the same meaning.

My friend Mary is very (1) social. She talks to everyone. Yesterday she talked during class. Mary's stories are always (2) humorous so everyone in class laughed. The teacher was (3) annoyed, and she did not laugh. She said Mary was (4) naughty and that she should behave in class. Mary (5) apologized. You could tell she was sorry. She was even able to stay (6) quiet and not make a sound . . . for 10 whole minutes!

1. ◯ friendly ◯ quiet   4. ◯ shy   ◯ impolite

2. ◯ angry   ◯ funny   5. ◯ silly   ◯ said sorry

3. ◯ upset   ◯ joyful   6. ◯ silent   ◯ tall

Just Like a Detective!

Detectives look for clues. You can also look for clues as long as you pay close attention!

Look at the pictures below. Use clues from the pictures to answer the questions.

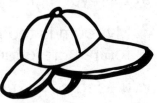

1. What has happened to make the little boy sad?

_____

_____

3. Are the two children friends? How can you tell?

_____

_____

2. Is the girl happy to be getting a present? How do you know?

_____

_____

4. How does this child feel? How can you tell?

_____

_____

Figure It Out

Complete each sentence with a word in the box. Use clues in each sentence to find the answer.

homework	friends	harder	walk	straight

1. Caroline and Kelsey are best _____ , and they do almost everything together.

2. English is easy to me, but math seems much _____ .

3. I don't like to run, but I do like to _____ to get exercise.

4. My mother has _____ hair. It will not curl at all.

5. My dog ate my _____ , so I can't get a grade.

What Happens When?

Most events happen in sequence or in order. Think about how your day usually goes. There are things you do in the morning, things you do in the middle of the day, and things you do each night.

Now read about Mr. Stickman's day. The events of his day are all mixed up. Use the words in the box to fill out his planner in the correct order.

go to bed	go to work	get ready for bed
get up	go home	eat supper
eat breakfast	eat lunch	

Mr. Stickman's Daily Planner

1. 6:00 A.M. _____

2. 6:30 A.M. _____

3. 8:00 A.M. _____

4. 1:00 P.M. _____

5. 5:00 P.M. _____

6. 6:30 P.M. _____

7. 8:00 P.M. _____

8. 9:00 P.M. _____

First, Second, Third

Read the story. Then number the events from the story.

Once there was a little girl named Jane. Jane was very sad. She wanted a puppy for her birthday. Her parents said she could not have a puppy. They had no place to keep a dog. Finally Jane's birthday arrived. There with the other presents was a box with holes all over the lid. The giant box had Jane's name on it. Jane opened the box and inside was a puppy. She was so happy. Her parents smiled and said the dog could stay inside the house. Jane was so happy because she finally got her birthday wish!

_____ Jane got her birthday wish.

_____ Jane wanted a puppy.

_____ Jane's parents said she could not have a puppy.

_____ Jane's birthday party finally arrived.

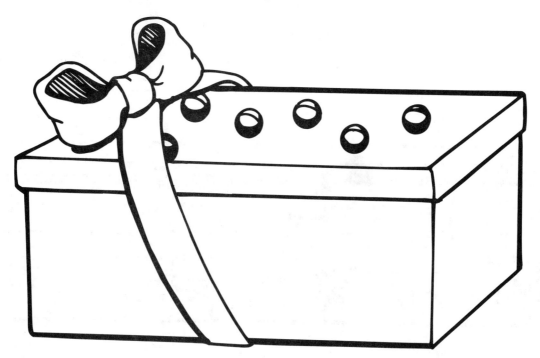

Grandma's Mix-Up

This story is all mixed up. See if you can rewrite the story in the order it should go.

I picked out a lizard.

We definitely had a wonderful day at the pet store!

Today my grandma took me to the pet store.

I named him Spikey.

After she paid for the lizard, I could not wait to get Spikey home.

At the pet store, Grandma said I could get a pet.

_____

_____

_____

_____

_____

_____

First, Next, Finally

Some words help us tell when things happened.

Look at each activity.

Write *first*, *next*, or *finally* in the order that things happened.

He put toothpaste on the toothbrush. _____

He rinsed out the toothpaste. _____

He brushed his teeth. _____

She tied her shoes. _____

She put her socks on her feet. _____

She put her shoes on her feet. _____

You put the pieces of bread together. _____

You put the peanut butter
and jelly on the bread. _____

You get out the bread,
the peanut butter, and the jelly. _____

What Comes First?

Look at the pictures.

Write 1 under what happened first.

Write 2 under what happened next.

Write 3 under what happened last.

1.

_____   _____   _____

2.

_____   _____   _____

66

It's All Connected

A cause is a reason why something happens. The effect is what happens after the cause.

A bad grade on your report card (the cause) may upset you (the effect). A good grade on your report card (the cause) may make you happy (the effect).

Look at the pictures below. Draw a line and match each cause to its effect.

Cause   **Effect**

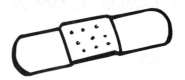

Because, Because

Complete each cause with an effect.

Example: She practices softball.

        The effect is <u>she will play well.</u>

1. He eats an apple every day.

The effect is _____

2. The baby takes lots of naps.

The effect is _____

3. The boy saves his money.

The effect is _____

4. The children play outside.

The effect is _____

5. The students listen in class.

The effect is _____

68

Can You Prove It?

A fact can be proven. An opinion cannot. An opinion is how someone feels or thinks about something.

Fact: Today is a school day.

Opinion: Today is the best day of the week.

List five facts about you.

Friday
May
11

1. _____

2. _____

3. _____

4. _____

5. _____

List one opinion about school.

1. _____

List one opinion about your birthday.

2. _____

List one opinion about pizza.

3. _____

List one opinion about cold weather.

4. _____

List one opinion about country music.

5. _____

Just the Facts

A fact can be proven. An opinion cannot be proven.

Write an *F* by each sentence that is a fact. Write an *O* by each sentence that is an opinion.

_____**1.** Fridays are always fun.

_____**2.** Green is the best color.

_____**3.** There are seven days in a week.

_____**4.** Ice cream must stay frozen or it will melt.

_____**5.** Vanilla ice cream is the best.

_____**6.** There are 12 months in a year.

_____**7.** The best month is February.

_____**8.** People need water to live.

_____**9.** Hot chocolate is delicious.

_____**10.** There are 10 problems on this sheet.

Are We Alike?

When we compare things, we tell how they are alike. When we contrast things, we tell how they are different.

Look at the pictures. Then answer the questions.

1. List two ways these animals are the same.

_____

_____

List two ways these animals are different.

_____

_____

2. List one way these shapes are the same.

_____

_____

List one way these shapes are different.

_____

_____

3. List two ways these figures are the same.

_____

_____

4. List one way these figures are different.

_____

_____

Alike and Different

When you compare and contrast things, you tell how they are alike and how they are different.

Look at the pictures below.

List three ways winter and summer compare or are alike.

Then list three ways winter and summer contrast or are different.

Winter	**Summer**

Compare

1. _____

2. _____

3. _____

Contrast

1. _____

2. _____

3. _____

The Twins

Read the paragraph. Then answer the questions.

Velvet and Vonda are twins. They are not identical twins. This means they do not look alike. Also, they do not always act the same. Velvet likes to ride horses. Vonda does not like to do things outdoors. Vonda would rather read a book than ride a horse. Velvet wants to be a veterinarian when she grows up. Vonda wants to be a librarian. There is one thing Velvet and Vonda do have in common. They both have the same birthday!

---

1. List two ways Velvet and Vonda are different.

_____

_____

2. List two ways Velvet and Vonda are the same.

_____

_____

Do You Know?

Read the paragraph below.

Janie likes cheese pizza. Her friend Bill likes pepperoni pizza. Janie and Bill ordered one pizza. The pizza had cheese only on four slices and pepperoni only on four slices. When they finished eating, there was one slice of cheese pizza left.

Circle the sentences that you know are true.

1. Janie hates sausage pizza.

2. Bill likes pepperoni pizza.

3. Bill and Janie have been friends for years.

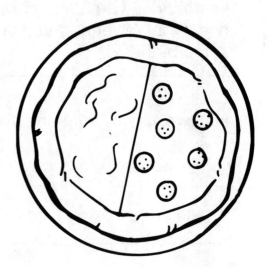

4. Bill paid for the pizza.

5. There was one slice of pizza left.

6. Janie ate less pizza than Bill.

7. Next time Janie and Bill will order hamburgers.

8. Janie and Bill's pizza had eight slices.

9. Only half of the pizza had pepperoni.

10. Janie doesn't really like pizza.

Figure It Out

Samuel lost his blue backpack. The last time he remembered seeing his backpack was on the bus. When Samuel got to school, he could not find his backpack anywhere. He asked his teacher, Mrs. Smith, if he could go to the office to look for it. When he got to the office, his backpack was waiting for him. Someone on his bus had brought it to the office. Samuel was so happy. He wished he knew who to thank for finding his backpack.

Read each question. Circle the correct answer.

1. Why did Samuel have to go to the office?
   a. He was sick.

   b. He lost his lunch money.

   c. He was trying to find his backpack.

   d. He was getting an award from the principal.

2. Which sentence best describes Samuel?
   a. He sometimes loses things.

   b. He is a very smart boy.

   c. His favorite color is blue.

   d. He really likes his teacher, Mrs. Smith.

3. How did Samuel feel when he found his backpack?
   a. He was upset.

   b. He was happy.

   c. He was scared.

   d. He was angry.

4. What would be a good title for this story?
   a. The Very Bad Day

   b. Samuel's Exciting Day at School

   c. The Principal's Office

   d. The Missing Backpack

Can You Believe It?

If an event or thing can really happen, then it is real.

Things that can't really happen are fantasy.

    Jack sleeps. (real)

    Jack sleeps like a log. (fantasy)

Read each set of sentences. Write an *F* by what is fantasy. Write an *R* by what is real.

1. _____ a. The water is cold.

   _____ b. The water froze and turned into diamonds.

2. _____ a. He bought a magic carpet at the mall.

   _____ b. He bought some tennis shoes at the mall.

3. _____ a. Kelly played in her room with her toys.

   _____ b. Kelly's toys played with each other when Kelly left the room.

4. _____ a. The man drove the car down the road.

   _____ b. When the car got tired, it stopped.

5. _____ a. The sun winked at me as the day ended.

   _____ b. The sun set as the day ended.

6. _____ a. My stomach growled loudly and said, "Feed me now!"

   _____ b. I decided to eat lunch an hour earlier than usual because I was so hungry.

7. _____ a. The snowflakes danced as they touched the cold winter ground.

   _____ b. The snowflakes were cold as I caught them in my hands.

8. _____ a. The little dog laughed as he chased the cat.

   _____ b. The cat meowed loudly as she ran from the dog.

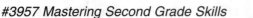

You Tell Me

Complete each sentence.

If the new sentence is real, color the sentence yellow.

If the new sentence is fantasy, do not color it.

1. My best friend _____.

2. The dog _____ in his doghouse.

3. When I order pizza, _____.

4. Every student _____.

5. The teacher _____.

Now draw a picture that is like one of your sentences.

Do You Know? Do You Know?

Wouldn't it be nice to have a magical crystal ball to be able to see what's going to happen next?

A good reader doesn't have to have a magic ball to make a guess or a prediction about what will happen next in a story. Pay close attention to the details and see if you can predict what will happen next.

Andy wants to hit a home run at his next baseball game. Every day he practices baseball with his dad. Each day he hits the ball better and better. Before the game begins, Andy feels sure he can hit a home run.

What do you think will happen at the game?

Circle the correct answer.

1.

   a. Andy will tell the coach he doesn't want to play.

   b. Andy will play very well during the game.

Maria and her brother Carl are both taking swimming lessons during the summer. Maria likes the water and is excited about the lessons. Carl is afraid of the water, but his swimming teacher is patient and nice. She tells Carl that each day he will learn a little more than the day before. By the third day, Carl is no longer afraid to get in the pool.

What do you think will happen next?

Circle the correct answer.

2.

   a. Carl will learn to swim.

   b. Maria will stop wanting to take swimming lessons.

Learn from What You Know

A good reader likes to predict what is going to happen next.

Read the sentences below.

Predict what will happen next.

Then write your answer.

1.

a. Kevin fixed himself a glass of juice.

b. Kevin spilled his glass of juice.

c. _____

2.

a. The Wilson family went out to eat.

b. The waitress took their order.

c. _____

3.

a. The man on the radio said there was snow on the way.

b. The temperature was below freezing, and the sky was filled with clouds.

c. _____

4.

a. Sandra had a spelling test on Friday.

b. On Thursday she practiced all the words and could spell each one.

c. _____

The Main Idea

A paragraph has sentences that are all about the same idea. There is one main idea, and there are other sentences to add more information about the main idea.

Example: School is fun. We get to play games. We learn many new things, and we also go outside to play.

The main idea is school is fun. The other sentences tell how or why school is fun.

Read each main idea.

List details to support the main idea.

1. Main idea: The zoo is a fun place to visit.

a. _____

b. _____

c. _____

2. Main idea: Summer is a fun season.

a. _____

b. _____

c. _____

3. Main idea: Second grade is better than first grade.

a. _____

b. _____

c. _____

4. Main idea: I am special.

a. _____

b. _____

c. _____

More of the Main Idea

The main idea or topic sentence is what a paragraph is all about.

The paragraphs below are missing a topic sentence.

Read each paragraph and look at your choices.

Then write the correct topic sentence.

1. _____

While we were there, we saw elephants, giraffes, and even a lion. Some of the animals, like the snakes and the lizards, were inside special buildings made just for them. Most of the animals were outside in the larger areas of the zoo. When it was time to leave, I was sad to go. I hope we get to have another field trip to the zoo soon.

a. We have been on five field trips this year.

b. Going to the zoo was fun.

c. I love animals.

2. _____

Everyone in my family was so scared. Only my little brother Scott likes snakes, so he had to get the snake out of the kitchen sink. We all stood in the next room and watched. Scott took a long stick and carefully put the snake back into the woods. We still don't know how the snake got in the sink, but I do know we were all glad Scott saved the day!

a. One day we found a snake in the kitchen sink.

b. Snakes are scary to some people.

c. My brother Scott likes snakes.

Putting Things in Order

A paragraph has more than one sentence. Each sentence in a paragraph is about the same topic. The first sentence, or topic sentence, will tell the main idea. The other sentences will give more information about the topic.

Read the sentences below.

Number each sentence in the order it should come in the paragraph.

A.

_____ His name is Rufus.

_____ My dog is a great pet.

_____ After we play, I pet him and tell him he's the greatest dog in the world!

_____ When Rufus and I play catch, he never misses the ball.

B.

_____ Then my new tree house was finally ready!

_____ First, my daddy said we had to get all the supplies.

_____ My daddy built me a tree house.

_____ Next, we had to get busy working.

The ABC's of Order

Place the following words in alphabetical order.

List A

candy

cake

chocolate

cookies

caramel

List B

puppy

penguin

pelican

parrot

panther

List C

Alicia

Alex

Ann

Allison

Amanda

List A

1. _____

2. _____

3. _____

4. _____

5. _____

List B

1. _____

2. _____

3. _____

4. _____

5. _____

List C

1. _____

2. _____

3. _____

4. _____

5. _____

Sweet Endings

Sometimes you can add a new ending to a word and make a whole new word.
Read each word and ending below. Then write the new word.

1. class + es

_____

6. greet + ed

_____

2. bus + es

_____

7. brush + es

_____

3. lean + ing

_____

8. heat + ed

_____

4. keep + ing

_____

9. sing + ing

_____

5. do + ing

_____

10. shout + ing

_____

84

Combining Words

Compound words are two words put together to make a new word.

Example: grand + parent = grandparent

Look at the drawings below. Then write the compound word that names each picture.

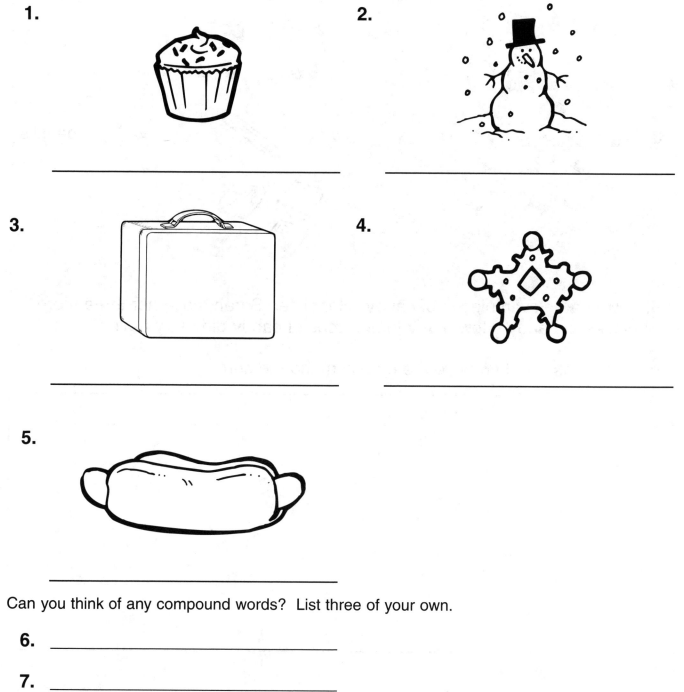

1.

_____

2.

_____

3.

_____

4.

_____

5.

_____

Can you think of any compound words? List three of your own.

6. _____

7. _____

8. _____

Colorful Addition

Count the pictures to find the sum.

1. [kittens]   +   [kittens]   = _____ kittens

2. [pigs]   +   [pigs]   = _____ pigs

3. [pencils]   +   [pencil]   = _____ pencils

4. [books]   +   [books]   = _____ books

5. Mary had eleven pieces of candy. Her sister, Sarah, gave her three more pieces of candy. How many total pieces of candy did Mary have?

Draw your answer, then write the equation and the sum.

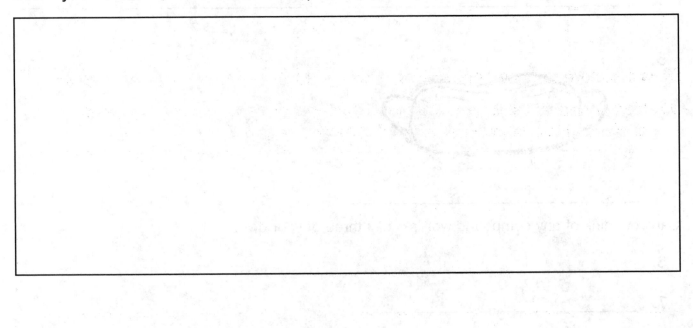

_____   +   _____   =   _____

Practice Makes Perfect

Add the numbers to find the sum.

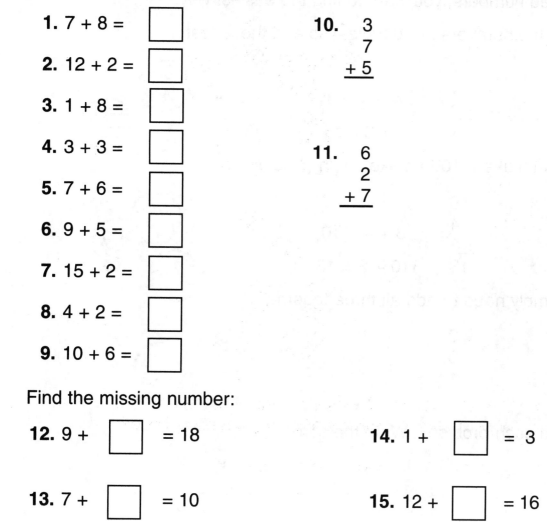

1. 7 + 8 = ☐

2. 12 + 2 = ☐

3. 1 + 8 = ☐

4. 3 + 3 = ☐

5. 7 + 6 = ☐

6. 9 + 5 = ☐

7. 15 + 2 = ☐

8. 4 + 2 = ☐

9. 10 + 6 = ☐

10.
$$\begin{array}{r} 3 \\ 7 \\ +\,5 \\ \hline \end{array}$$

11.
$$\begin{array}{r} 6 \\ 2 \\ +\,7 \\ \hline \end{array}$$

Find the missing number:

12. 9 + ☐ = 18

13. 7 + ☐ = 10

14. 1 + ☐ = 3

15. 12 + ☐ = 16

Draw a picture to show the answer. Then write the equation and the answer.

16. Sandy had two suckers. She went to the store and bought five more suckers. How many suckers did she have in all?

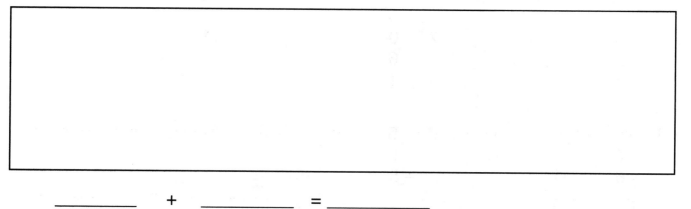

_____ + _____ = _____

Finding the Easiest Way

When you add three numbers, you want to find the easiest way.

Sometimes two of the numbers are doubles, so add these first.

$$\begin{array}{r} 4 \\ 4 \\ +\,3 \\ \hline 11 \end{array}$$ 4 + 4 = 8

8 + 3 = 11

Sometimes you can make a 10 to make adding easier.

$$\begin{array}{r} 6 \\ 4 \\ +\,3 \\ \hline 13 \end{array}$$ 6 + 4 = 10

10 + 3 = 13

Sometimes you simply need to add all three together.

$$\begin{array}{r} 2 \\ 3 \\ +\,1 \\ \hline 6 \end{array}$$

Decide how to add each problem. Write the sum.

1. $\begin{array}{r} 7 \\ 2 \\ +\,3 \\ \hline \end{array}$	**5.** $\begin{array}{r} 1 \\ 9 \\ +\,3 \\ \hline \end{array}$	**9.** $\begin{array}{r} 2 \\ 8 \\ +\,8 \\ \hline \end{array}$
2. $\begin{array}{r} 3 \\ 6 \\ +\,3 \\ \hline \end{array}$	**6.** $\begin{array}{r} 9 \\ 3 \\ +\,2 \\ \hline \end{array}$	**10.** $\begin{array}{r} 9 \\ 9 \\ +\,0 \\ \hline \end{array}$
3. $\begin{array}{r} 4 \\ 2 \\ +\,3 \\ \hline \end{array}$	**7.** $\begin{array}{r} 0 \\ 6 \\ +\,1 \\ \hline \end{array}$	**11.** $\begin{array}{r} 8 \\ 3 \\ +\,2 \\ \hline \end{array}$
4. $\begin{array}{r} 4 \\ 2 \\ +\,6 \\ \hline \end{array}$	**8.** $\begin{array}{r} 5 \\ 5 \\ +\,5 \\ \hline \end{array}$	**12.** $\begin{array}{r} 2 \\ 7 \\ +\,1 \\ \hline \end{array}$

Regroup for Addition

7 + 8 = 15

There is 1 ten.

There are 5 ones.

Add each problem.

Write how many tens.

Write how many ones.

	Tens	Ones
1. 7 + 9 = ☐		
2. 4 + 7 = ☐		
3. 3 + 8 = ☐		
4. 9 + 5 = ☐		
5. 6 + 6 = ☐		

Answer each question.

6. 17 is made up of ☐ ten and ☐ ones.

7. 12 is made up of ☐ ten and ☐ ones.

8. 14 is made up of ☐ ten and ☐ ones.

Double Take

Knowing the sum of doubles helps you add faster.

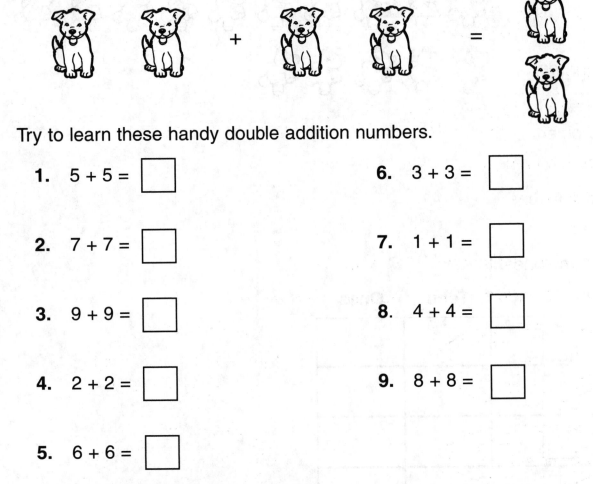

Try to learn these handy double addition numbers.

1. 5 + 5 = ☐

2. 7 + 7 = ☐

3. 9 + 9 = ☐

4. 2 + 2 = ☐

5. 6 + 6 = ☐

6. 3 + 3 = ☐

7. 1 + 1 = ☐

8. 4 + 4 = ☐

9. 8 + 8 = ☐

Read the problem. Draw the doubles. Find the sum.

10. Sarah has five red balloons. Her friend Andre has five blue balloons. How many balloons do they have in all?

☐ + ☐ = ☐

Easy as Pie!

When you learn to add doubles, adding one more makes finding the right answer as easy as pie!

5 + 5 = 10

a double equation

5 + 6 = 11

a double equation plus 1

All you do is add 1!

Find the sums.

Color each double addition equation blue.

Color each double addition plus 1 equation yellow.

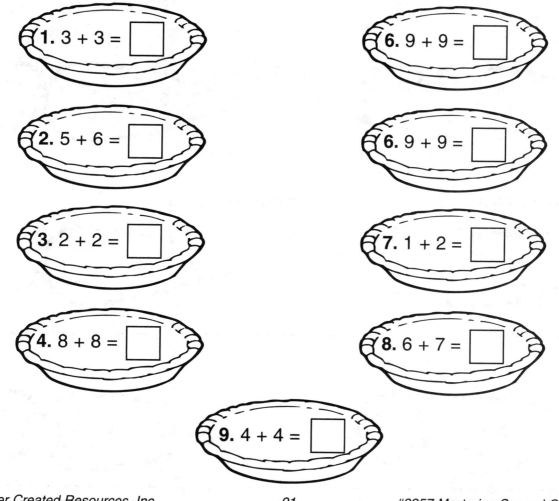

1. 3 + 3 =

2. 5 + 6 =

3. 2 + 2 =

4. 8 + 8 =

6. 9 + 9 =

6. 9 + 9 =

7. 1 + 2 =

8. 6 + 7 =

9. 4 + 4 =

Hop to It

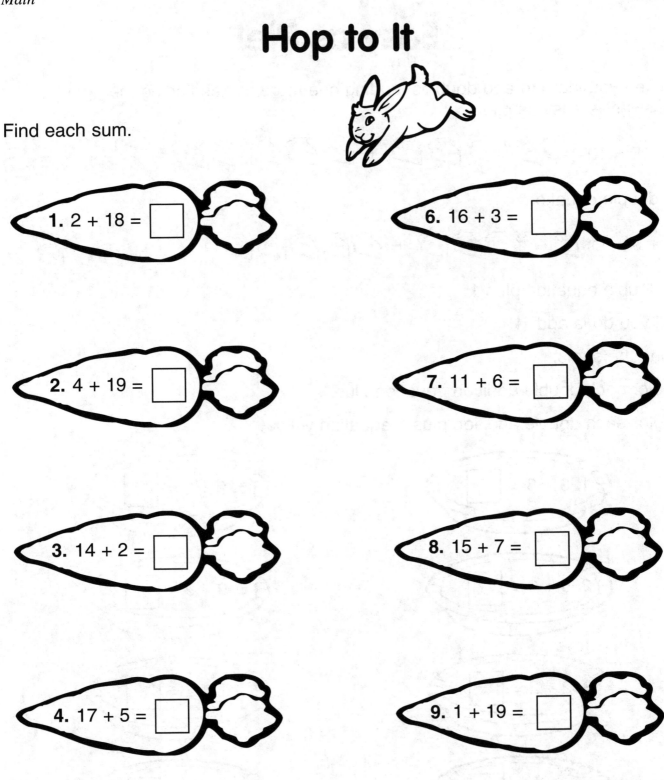

Find each sum.

1. 2 + 18 = ☐

2. 4 + 19 = ☐

3. 14 + 2 = ☐

4. 17 + 5 = ☐

5. 8 + 12 = ☐

6. 16 + 3 = ☐

7. 11 + 6 = ☐

8. 15 + 7 = ☐

9. 1 + 19 = ☐

10. 13 + 4 = ☐

Double the Fun

Add each line of two-digit numbers.

1. 30
+12

4. 18
+16

7. 20
+10

10. 24
+19

2. 46
+30

5. 27
+34

8. 48
+42

11. 29
+18

3. 17
+22

6. 16
+12

9. 53
+37

12. 61
+22

13. Amanda has 20 pennies. Her cousin Melissa gives her 23 pennies. How many total pennies does Amanda have now?

☐ pennies

14. Katherine has 12 toys. Her brother Braden has 11 toys. How many toys do they have together?

☐ toys

Triple the Fun

Find each sum.

| **1.** 675 | **4.** 851 | **7.** 729 | **10.** 243 |
| + 321 | +123 | +148 | +213 |

| **2.** 235 | **5.** 463 | **8.** 581 | **11.** 712 |
| +102 | +333 | +401 | +202 |

| **3.** 134 | **6.** 102 | **9.** 900 | **12.** 623 |
| +100 | +101 | +100 | +317 |

Now it's your turn!

In the space below, create three addition problems of your own. Remember, each number should have three digits. When you are finished, have another student answer your problems.

13.   **14.**   **15.**

+   +   +
_____   _____   _____

Practice, Practice, Practice

Practice your addition by adding these three-digit numbers.

1. 444
+132

4. 821
+123

7. 321
+231

2. 555
+264

5. 871
+112

8. 899
+100

3. 789
+100

6. 412
+402

9. 222
+444

Solve each addition problem.

10. Cassidy has 123 pennies. Her friend Todd has 112 pennies. How many pennies do they have together?

_____ + _____ = _____

11. Ken has 312 trading cards. On his birthday his parents give him 200 more. How many trading cards does Ken have now?

_____ + _____ = _____

12. Last summer Ruth and Ruby planted 112 flowers. This summer their friends Pat and Ann helped them plant 100 more. How many flowers do they have now?

_____ + _____ = _____

Figure It Out!

Solve the two-digit subtraction problems to find the secret message.

1. 23 −12	**3.** 29 −21	**5.** 65 −35	**7.** 48 −38
C	U	L	Y

2. 57 −43	**4.** 77 −60	**6.** 18 −13	**8.** 38 −10
O	A	E	R

___   ___   ___   ___   ___   ___   ___   ___   ___   ___

10   14   8   17   28   5   11   14   14   30

Practice Makes Perfect

Practice these three-digit subtraction problems.

1. 342
-234

5. 777
-189

9. 750
-570

13. 853
-400

2. 478
-300

6. 213
-143

10. 588
-189

14. 573
-100

3. 987
-465

7. 510
-428

11. 799
-700

15. 876
-487

4. 651
-543

8. 148
-111

12. 733
-555

16. 444
-222

4 5 6

It's All in the Family

A fact family is a group of numbers in subtraction and addition that use the same numbers.

Subtract and add these fact family problems.

1.

7 + 3 = ☐

10 − 3 = ☐

2.

6 + 8 = ☐

14 − 8 = ☐

3.

6 + 6 = ☐

12 − 6 = ☐

4.

4 + 7 = ☐

11 − 7 = ☐

5.

9 + 8 = ☐

17 − 8 = ☐

6.

1 + 2 = ☐

3 − 2 = ☐

What's Missing?

Find the missing number in each addition problem.

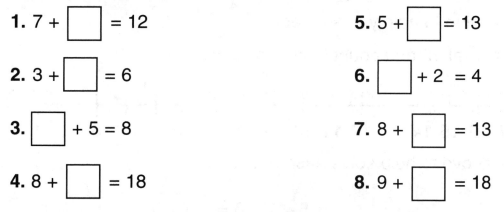

1. 7 + ☐ = 12

2. 3 + ☐ = 6

3. ☐ + 5 = 8

4. 8 + ☐ = 18

5. 5 + ☐ = 13

6. ☐ + 2 = 4

7. 8 + ☐ = 13

8. 9 + ☐ = 18

Find the missing number in each subtraction problem.

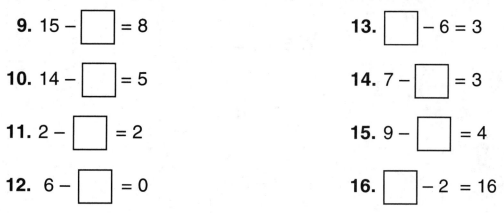

9. 15 − ☐ = 8

10. 14 − ☐ = 5

11. 2 − ☐ = 2

12. 6 − ☐ = 0

13. ☐ − 6 = 3

14. 7 − ☐ = 3

15. 9 − ☐ = 4

16. ☐ − 2 = 16

Solve the story problem.

17. Carlos had five apples in a sack. He met some of his friends at the park. At the park he gave away some of his apples. When he got home, he had one apple left.

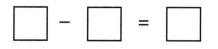

☐ − ☐ = ☐

Write an equation showing how many apples Carlos gave away and how many he kept.

A Help Line for Subtraction

One way to make subtraction easier is to use a number line.

You can use a number line to help you subtract.

To subtract 12 − 7, start at 12 and count backward 7 spaces.

12 − 7 = 5

20 19 18 17 16 15 14 13 12 11 10 9 8 7 6 5 4 3 2 1

Use the number line above to help solve each equation.

1. 18 − 2 = ☐

2. 12 − 11 = ☐

3. 17 − 1 = ☐

4. 8 − 5 = ☐

5. 18 − 17 = ☐

6. 15 − 6 = ☐

7. 5 − 3 = ☐

8. 16 − 10 = ☐

9. 17 − 8 = ☐

10. 7 − 4 = ☐

Use the number line to find the answer.

11. 12 − 5 =

○ 6   ○ 7

○ 5   ○ 17

12. 10 - 3 =

○ 4   ○ 2

○ 7   ○ 5

Seeing Double

Start at the number 2 and count by two's to discover the hidden pictures.

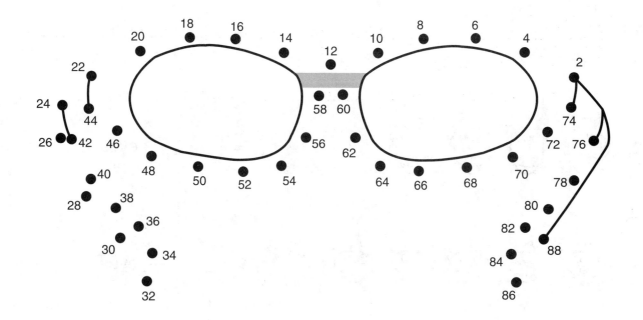

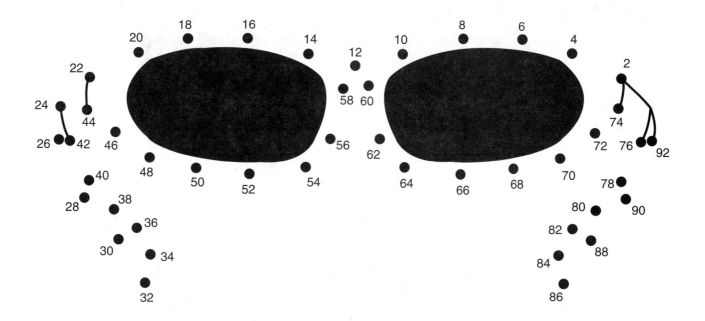

Out of This World

Aliens with three eyes have invaded your worksheet!

Count the eyes on each alien by three's to find the number of eyes that are watching you.

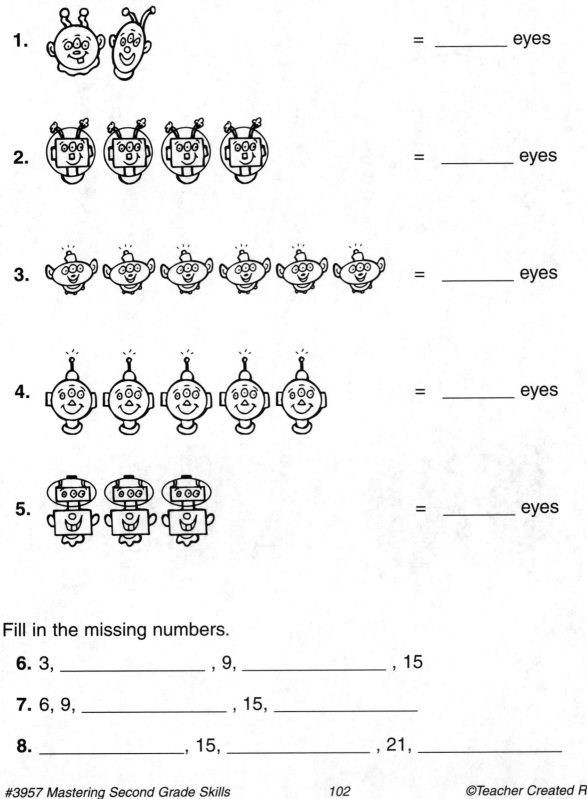

1. = _____ eyes

2. = _____ eyes

3. = _____ eyes

4. = _____ eyes

5. = _____ eyes

Fill in the missing numbers.

6. 3, _____ , 9, _____ , 15

7. 6, 9, _____ , 15, _____

8. _____ , 15, _____ , 21, _____

Five, Ten, Fifteen, Twenty

Circle the things that you can count by five's.

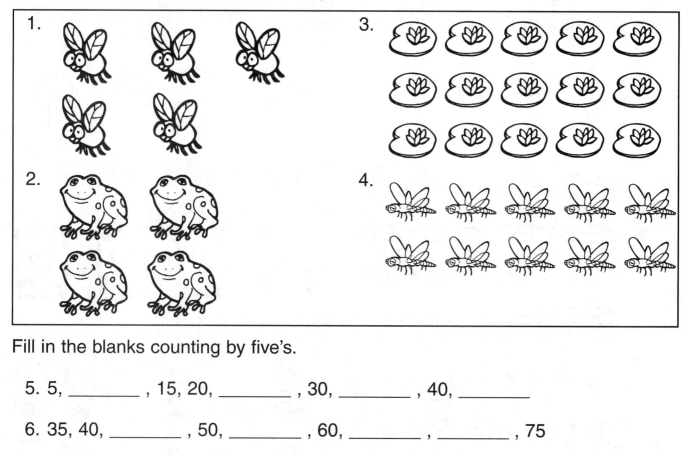

Fill in the blanks counting by five's.

5. 5, _____ , 15, 20, _____ , 30, _____ , 40, _____

6. 35, 40, _____ , 50, _____ , 60, _____ , _____ , 75

7. 5, _____ , 15, _____ , _____ , _____ , _____ , _____

In the space below, draw five circles, five triangles, and five squares.

How many items did you draw? _____

Pick Which One

Look at each group of items.

Circle the group that can be counted by five's.

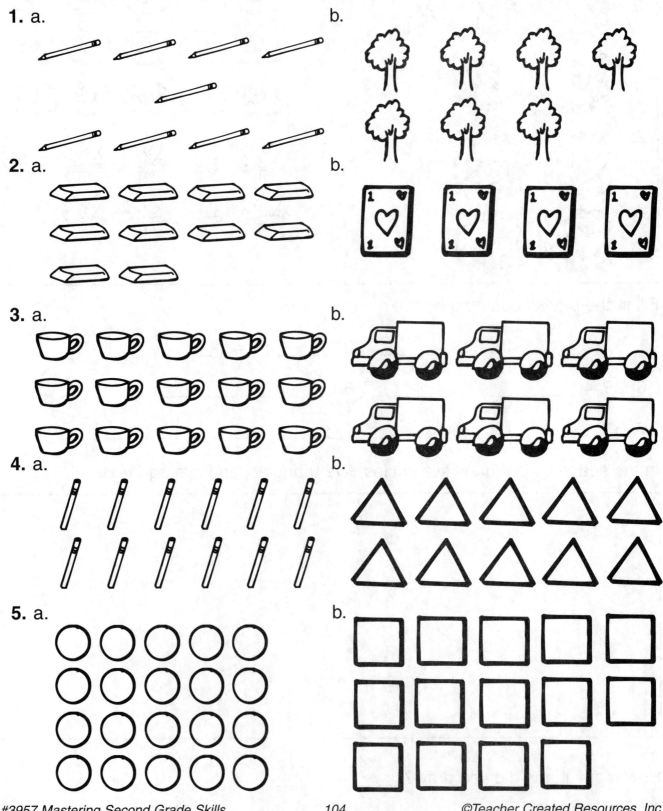

1. a.   b.

2. a.   b.

3. a.   b.

4. a.   b.

5. a.   b.

The Ants Go Marching

There are 10 ones in the number 10.

1 + 1 + 1 + 1 + 1 + 1 + 1 + 1 + 1 + 1 = 10

Circle the things at the picnic that are in groups of 10.

The Happy Tens

Counting by ten's is quick and easy. Things that are quick and easy make people smile. Remember that 1 ten = 10 ones. Count the happy faces.

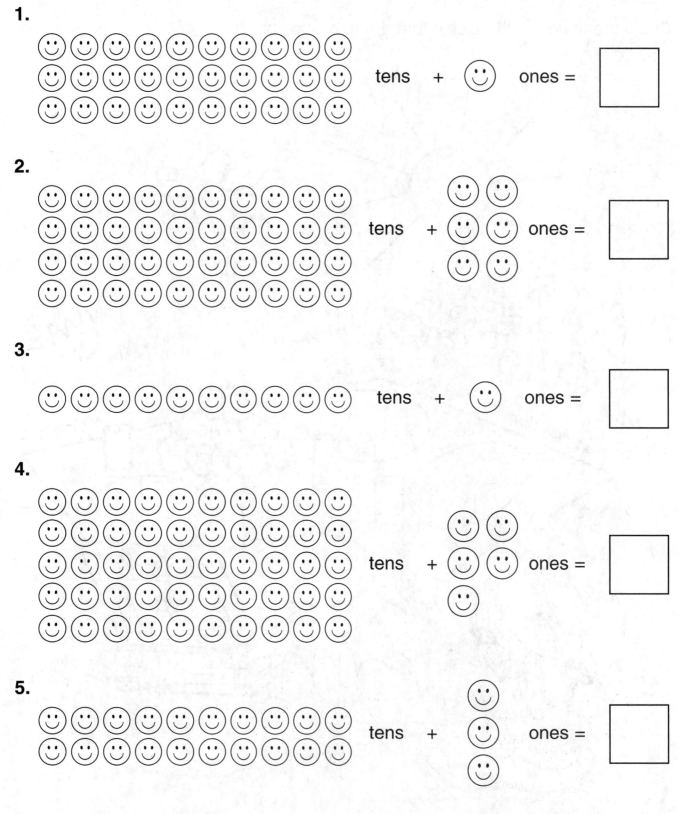

1.
＿＿＿ tens + ☺ ones = ☐

2.
＿＿＿ tens + ☺☺☺☺ ones = ☐

3.
＿＿＿ tens + ☺ ones = ☐

4.
＿＿＿ tens + ☺☺☺☺☺ ones = ☐

5.
＿＿＿ tens + ☺☺☺ ones = ☐

What Comes Next?

Count by ten's to find what comes next.

1. 10, 20, 30, _____

2. 50, 60, 70, _____

3. 20, 30, 40, _____

4. 70, 80, 90, _____

Count by ten's to find the missing numbers.

5. 10, _____, 30, 40, _____, 60, _____

6. _____, 50, 60, _____, 80, _____, 100

7. 40, _____, 60, _____, 80, _____

8. Carole Ann has 10 snails. Rhonda has 20 worms. Their friend Robert has 10 lizards. How many creepy crawlies do they have in all?

$$\boxed{} + \boxed{} + \boxed{} = \boxed{}$$

Counting Backward

To count by ten's backward, subtract 10 each time.

Examples:	
35, 25, 15, 5	44, 34, 24, 14

Count backward by ten's to complete the pattern.

1. 52, _____ , 32, 22,

2. 70, 60, _____ , _____

3. 62, 52, _____ , 32

4. 91, _____ , 71, _____

5. 85, 75, _____ , 55

6. 43, _____ , 23, _____

7. 75, _____ , _____ , 45

8. 97, _____ , 77, _____

Find each difference.

9. $50 - 40 =$ ☐

10. $44 - 34 =$ ☐

11. $95 - 85 =$ ☐

12. $75 - 65 =$ ☐

Like Shoes and Socks

Even numbers are when you count by two's. These numbers can form pairs just like your shoes do!

2, 4, 6, 8, and 10 are all even numbers.

Odd numbers do not form pairs. Odd numbers are like socks with no mates. Odd numbers come between even numbers.

1, 3, 5, 7, and 11 are all odd numbers.

Look at each number below. If the number is even, circle it. If the number is odd, write an X on it.

1. 6	**6.** 11
2. 7	**7.** 4
3. 15	**8.** 9
4. 1	**9.** 2
5. 8	**10.** 5

11. List two things that can come in even numbers.

Example: a person's hands

_____   _____

12. List two things that can come in odd numbers

Example: birthday candles for a 7th birthday

_____   _____

Guess How Many

When you estimate, you guess how many are in a group.

1. Estimate how many students are in your class.

2. Estimate how many desks are in your class.

3. Estimate how many students are wearing tennis shoes.

4. Estimate how many students have lunch boxes.

5. Estimate how many marbles are in the jar.

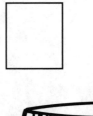

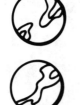

Like Stars in the Sky

Like stars in the sky, some things are too hard to count exactly. That is when you need to estimate. When you estimate, you are guessing how many of something you think there is instead of counting every single thing. Estimate the number of stars in each group. Circle your answer. Use these groups to help you estimate.

10 stars	30 stars	50 stars

1. ○ 10   ○ 30   ○ 50

2. ○ 10   ○ 30   ○ 50

3. ○ 10   ○ 30   ○ 50

4. ○ 10   ○ 30   ○ 50

5. ○ 10   ○ 30   ○ 50

6. On the back of this page draw a picture with stars in the sky. Ask a student to estimate how many stars are in your picture.

Less or More?

Some numbers are less than other numbers.
For example, 4 is less than 5.

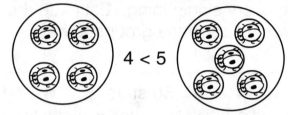

Some numbers are greater than other numbers.
For example, 5 is greater than 4.

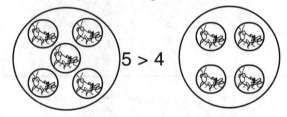

Look at each set. Then write > (greater than) or < (less than) on the line.

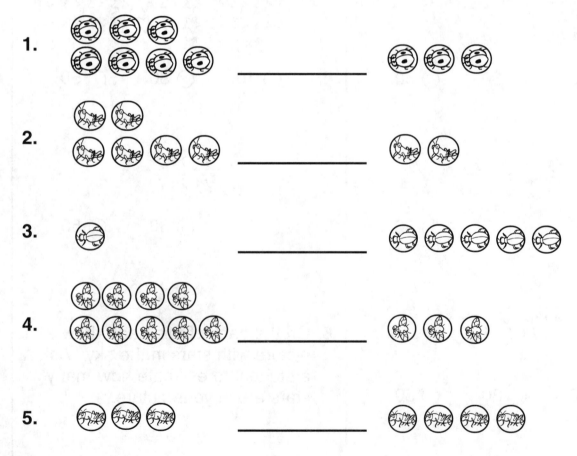

1.

2.

3.

4.

5.

Compare Those Numbers

Some numbers are larger than other numbers. Some numbers are smaller than other numbers. To compare numbers, use the greater than (>) or less than (<) sign.

Write the letter *G* over the number that is greater.

Write the letter *L* over the number that is less.

Write < or > on the line provided.

1. 23 _____ 32

5. 10 _____ 100

2. 18 _____ 81

6. 26 _____ 27

3. 45 _____ 12

7. 76 _____ 62

4. 30 _____ 40

8. 17 _____ 11

9. Draw a picture of pencils that shows greater than five pencils.

10. Draw a picture of fish that shows less than 10 fish.

After, Before, Between

Look at the number line.

You can see the number 3 comes after the number 2.

The number 2 comes before the number 3.

The number 2 comes between numbers 1 and 3.

Write the number that is before, after, or between.

1. 6 _____ 8   **3.** 12 _____ 14

2. 56 57 _____   **4.** _____ 35 36

Color the number squares that come before 15 blue.

Color the number squares that come after 15 yellow.

1	2	3	4	5	6	7	8	9	10
11	12	13	14	15	16	17	18	19	20
21	22	23	24	25	26	27	28	29	30

Ready, Set, Go

Write the position of the runners.

Example: Kelly: First, 1st

1. Crede _____

2. Dan _____

3. Sandy _____

4. Riley _____

5. Mike _____

School Years

Below are pictures of Cindy Lou in elementary school.

Color each picture. Then write the correct ordinal for each picture.

1. Cindy Lou in Mrs. Jones's fifth grade class

_____ grade

2. Cindy Lou sitting at her desk in first grade

_____ grade

3. Cindy Lou at the playground in third grade

_____ grade

4. Cindy Lou in fourth grade

_____ grade

Color Me Perfect

Look at each line of pictures.

Color every 1st picture green.

Color every 3rd picture purple.

Color every 5th picture red.

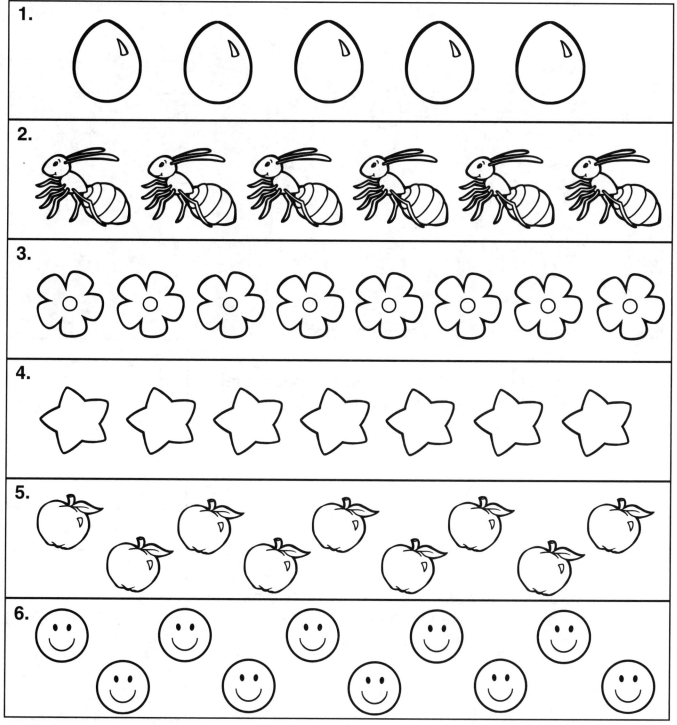

Keep the Change

Find the total amount.

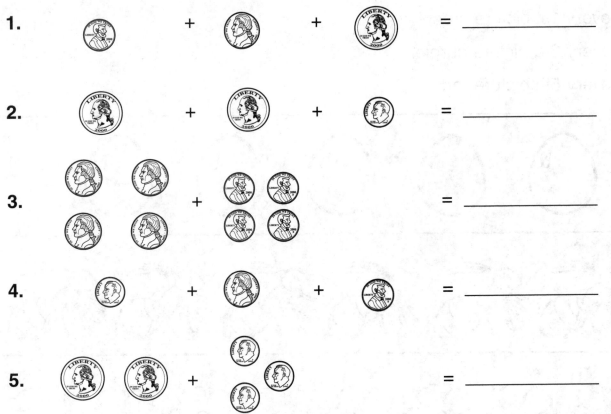

1. 　　　　+ 　　　　+ 　　　　= _____

2. 　　　　+ 　　　　+ 　　　　= _____

3. 　　　　+ 　　　　= _____

4. 　　　　+ 　　　　+ 　　　　= _____

5. 　　　　+ 　　　　= _____

Draw the coins to solve the following problems:

6. Tristan has two quarters, one dime, and one nickel. How much money does he have?

_____

7. Micah had three dimes, four nickels, and five pennies. How much money does she have?

_____

Purchase, Please

Circle the coins to show the price of each item.

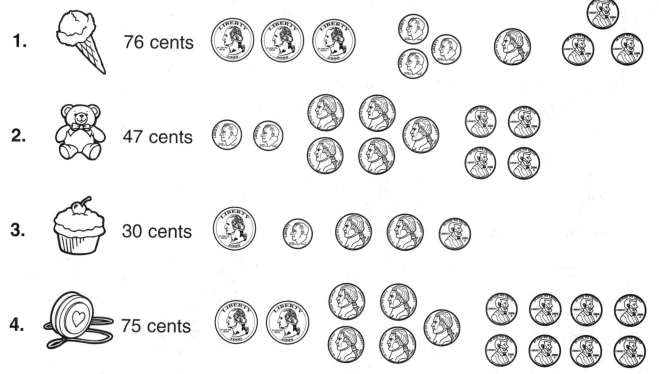

1. 76 cents

2. 47 cents

3. 30 cents

4. 75 cents

5. Marcie wants to buy a toy that costs 50 cents.

Draw the coins she would need.

Window Shopping

Circle the square that shows the correct amount of coins needed to buy the treat listed.

1. The amount needed for the cupcake:

24¢

2. The amount needed for the donut:

55¢

3. The amount needed for the dozen chocolate chip cookies:

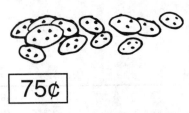

75¢

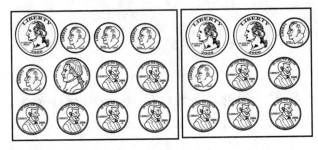

4. If you have one nickel already, how many quarters do you need to buy the donut?

_____

_____

5. Look at the cinnamon roll. How much money would you need to buy one?

67¢

How many dimes? _____

How many nickels? _____

How many pennies? _____

How Much Money?

Write the amount.

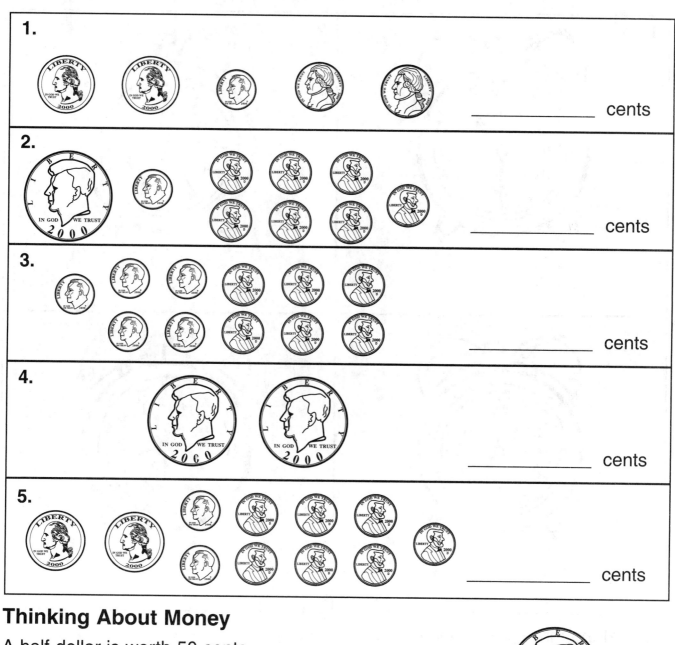

1.	_____ cents
2.	_____ cents
3.	_____ cents
4.	_____ cents
5.	_____ cents

Thinking About Money

A half-dollar is worth 50 cents.

List three things you could buy if you had 2 half-dollars:

1. _____

2. _____

3. _____

Looking at the Clock

Write the time shown on each clock.

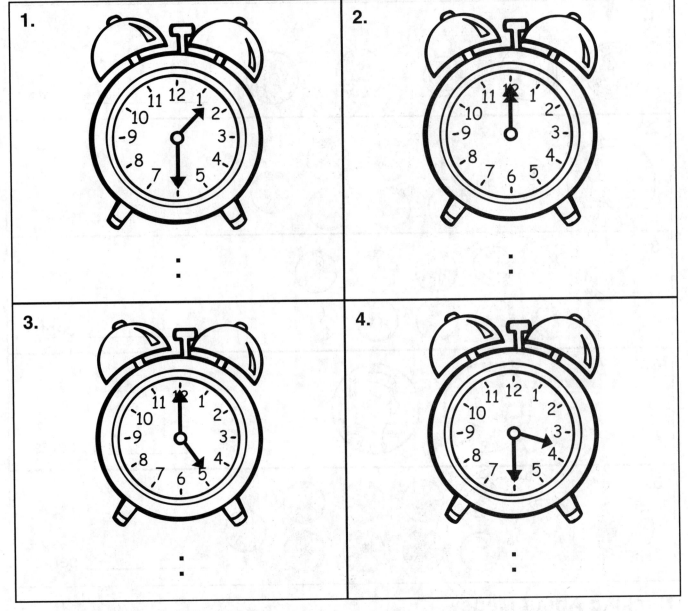

1.   :

2.   :

3.   :

4.   :

Look at the three clocks below.

Circle the clock that is closest to the time you go to bed.

The Mice Ran Up the Clock

Write the time shown on each clock.

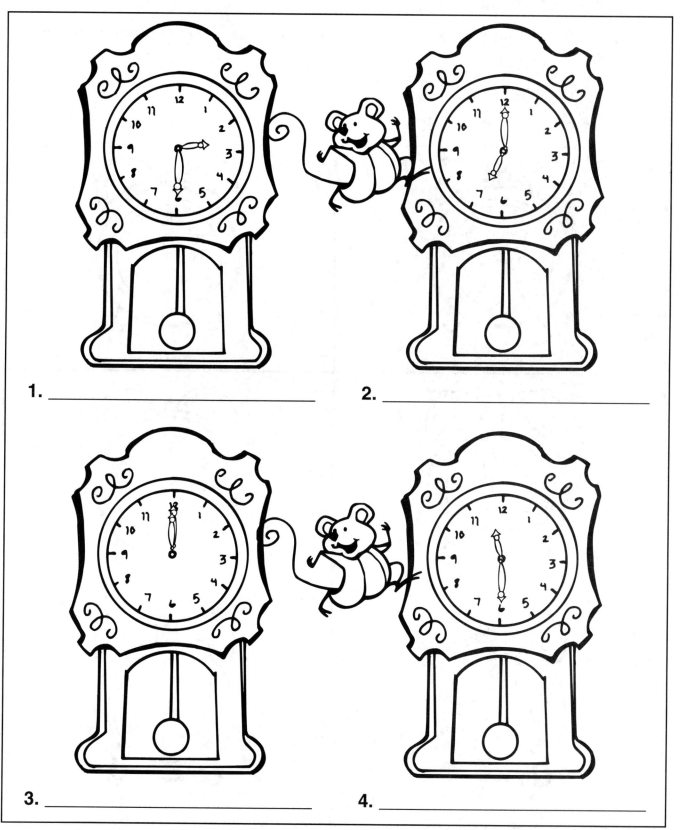

1. _____

2. _____

3. _____

4. _____

Learning More About Time

You can tell time if you can count by five's. Counting by five's will help you tell the minutes after the hour.

The time is 9:10. You counted by five's to decide how many minutes there are after 9:00.

Look at each clock.

Write the time below the clock.

What Time Is Your Time?

Each day you do things at special times.

Look at each blank clock.

Draw the hour hand and the minute hand to show what time you usually do each thing.

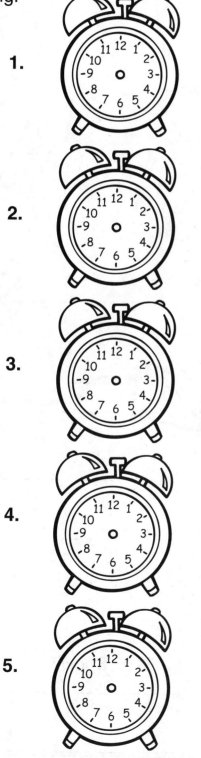

1.   This is the time I get up each morning.

2.   This is the time I leave for school.

3.   This is the time I eat lunch.

4.   This is the time I eat dinner.

5.   This is the time I go to sleep.

A Timely Festival

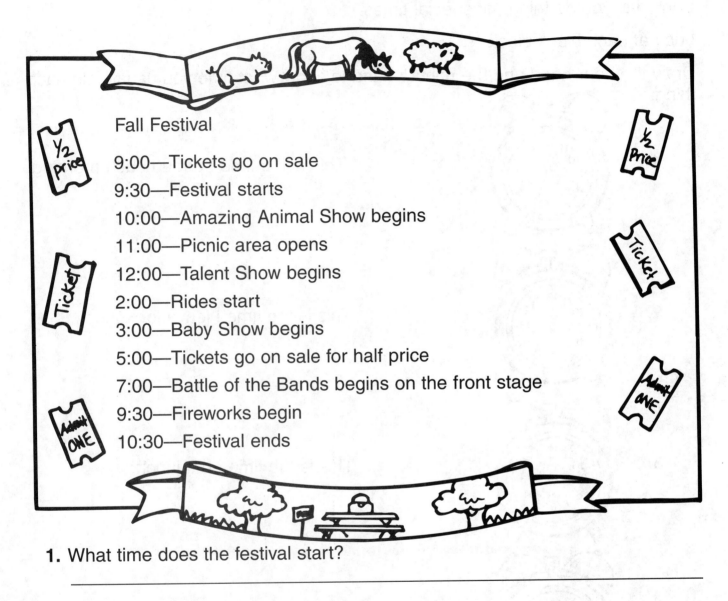

Fall Festival

9:00—Tickets go on sale

9:30—Festival starts

10:00—Amazing Animal Show begins

11:00—Picnic area opens

12:00—Talent Show begins

2:00—Rides start

3:00—Baby Show begins

5:00—Tickets go on sale for half price

7:00—Battle of the Bands begins on the front stage

9:30—Fireworks begin

10:30—Festival ends

1. What time does the festival start?

_____

2. When does the last event begin?

_____

3. Which one begins first, the Animal Show or the Baby Show?

_____

What time does it start?_____

4. How much time is between the Animal Show and the Baby Show?

_____

5. How long is the festival?

_____

Other Ways to Look at Time

A clock is not the only way you can look at time.

You can also use a calendar to show how time passes. A calendar will not show the hours and the minutes, but it will show the seven days of the week. It will also show the 12 months of the year and how many days are in each month.

♡ **FEBRUARY** ♡

SUN	MON	TUES	WED	THURS	FRI	SAT
	1	2	3	4	5	6
7	8	9	10	11	12	13
14	15	16	17	18	19	20
21	22	23	24	25	26	27
28						

Look at the calendar page.

1. Draw a circle around the part that shows what month it is.

2. Draw a triangle around the word that shows it is the first day of the week.

3. Draw a star in the square that shows the first day of the month.

4. Draw a rectangle in the square that shows the last day of the month.

5. Find the square that shows it is February 19. Color this square blue.

6. Find each square that shows a Saturday. Color these squares yellow.

Twelve Months Make a Year

Look at the calendar for the year and answer the questions below.

January

Sun	Mo	Tu	We	Th	Fr	Sa
1	2	3	4	5	6	7
8	9	10	11	12	13	14
15	16	17	18	19	20	21
22	23	24	25	26	27	28
29	30	31				

February

Sun	Mo	Tu	We	Th	Fr	Sa
			1	2	3	4
5	6	7	8	9	10	11
12	13	14	15	16	17	18
19	20	21	22	23	24	25
26	27	28				

March

Sun	Mo	Tu	We	Th	Fr	Sa
			1	2	3	4
5	6	7	8	9	10	11
12	13	14	15	16	17	18
19	20	21	22	23	24	25
26	27	28	29	30	31	

April

Sun	Mo	Tu	We	Th	Fr	Sa
						1
2	3	4	5	6	7	8
9	10	11	12	13	14	15
16	17	18	19	20	21	22
23	24	25	26	27	28	29
30						

May

Sun	Mo	Tu	We	Th	Fr	Sa
	1	2	3	4	5	6
7	8	9	10	11	12	13
14	15	16	17	18	19	20
21	22	23	24	25	26	27
28	29	30	31			

June

Sun	Mo	Tu	We	Th	Fr	Sa
				1	2	3
4	5	6	7	8	9	10
11	12	13	14	15	16	17
18	19	20	21	22	23	24
25	26	27	28	29	30	

July

Sun	Mo	Tu	We	Th	Fr	Sa
						1
2	3	4	5	6	7	8
9	10	11	12	13	14	15
16	17	18	19	20	21	22
23	24	25	26	27	28	29
30	31					

August

Sun	Mo	Tu	We	Th	Fr	Sa
		1	2	3	4	5
6	7	8	9	10	11	12
13	14	15	16	17	18	19
20	21	22	23	24	25	26
27	28	29	30	31		

September

Sun	Mo	Tu	We	Th	Fr	Sa
					1	2
3	4	5	6	7	8	9
10	11	12	13	14	15	16
17	18	19	20	21	22	23
24	25	26	27	28	29	30

October

Sun	Mo	Tu	We	Th	Fr	Sa
1	2	3	4	5	6	7
8	9	10	11	12	13	14
15	16	17	18	19	20	21
22	23	24	25	26	27	28
29	30	31				

November

Sun	Mo	Tu	We	Th	Fr	Sa
			1	2	3	4
5	6	7	8	9	10	11
12	13	14	15	16	17	18
19	20	21	22	23	24	25
26	27	28	29	30		

December

Sun	Mo	Tu	We	Th	Fr	Sa
					1	2
3	4	5	6	7	8	9
10	11	12	13	14	15	16
17	18	19	20	21	22	23
24	25	26	27	28	29	30
31						

1. How many days are in a week?

_____

2. How many months are in a year?

_____

3. How many months have 30 days?

_____

4. What is the first month of the year?

_____

5. What month is your birthday month?

_____

6. Which month comes before April?

_____

7. Which month comes after July?

_____

8. Which month has the fewest days?

_____

Calculating Time

Use a calculator to help you find the answers.

1. Karen left her friend's party at 5:00.

She arrived at the party at 3:00.

How many hours did she stay at the party?

____ hours

2. Today is Irene's birthday.

She is leaving for a trip in five days.

On what date will she leave for her trip? _____

3. Macey wakes up at 7:00.

She gets to school two hours later.

What time does she get to school? _____

4. Rhonda has dance class on Monday, October 1.

Her next class will be Monday, October 8.

How many days until she has class again?

_____ days

5. September has 30 days.

October has 31 days.

How many days total do September and October have?

_____ days

6. Betsy's ball practice starts at 4:00.

Practice ends at 6:00.

How many hours does Betsy have practice?_____ hours

Tally Marks

You can count objects by using tally marks.

| How many hearts are there? |

Use tally marks to show how many are in each group.

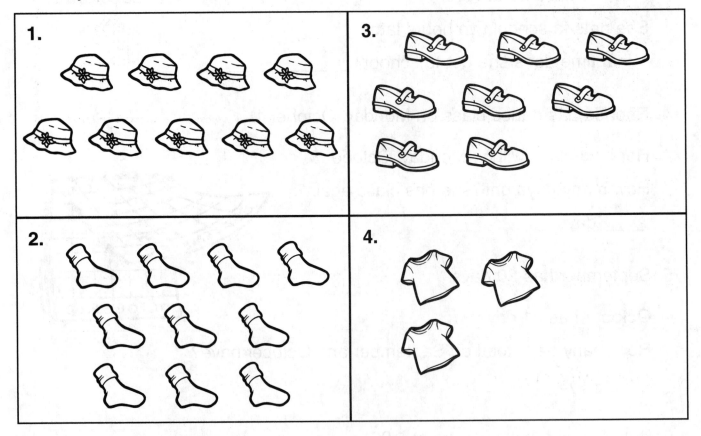

5. Use tally marks to show how many school books you have. _____

6. Use tally marks to show how many days are in a week. _____

Where Do You Like to Travel?

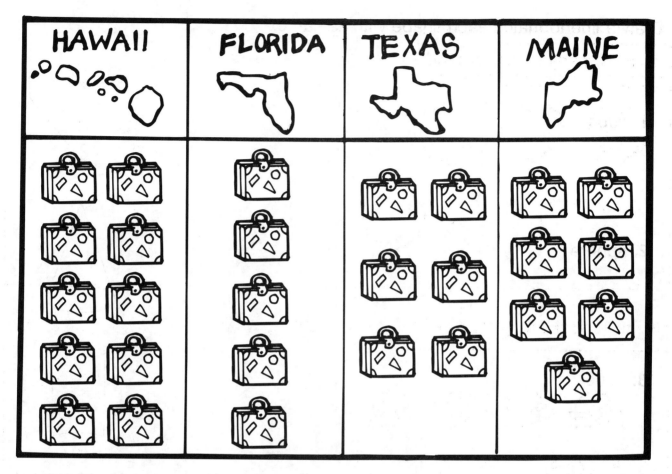

Use the graph to answer the questions.

1. Which state is the favorite vacation place?

   _____

2. Which state is the second least favorite vacation place?

   _____

3. Which two states are the least popular vacation places?

   _____

4. Which state would you most like to visit? Why?

   _____

Match the Shape

Draw a line to match each shape with its name.

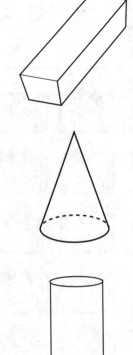

1. cube

2. sphere

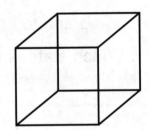

3. cone

4. rectangular prism

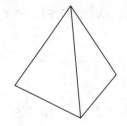

5. cylinder

6. pyramid

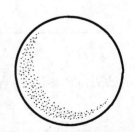

Looking Around

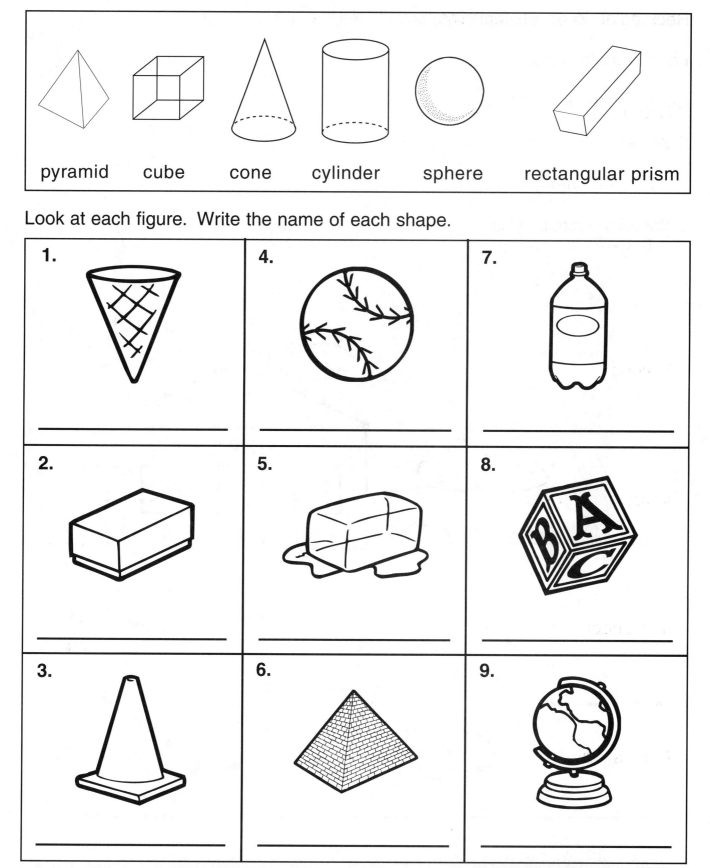

pyramid   cube   cone   cylinder   sphere   rectangular prism

Look at each figure. Write the name of each shape.

1.	**4.**	**7.**
2.	**5.**	**8.**
3.	**6.**	**9.**

The Plane! The Plane!

Rectangles, squares, triangles, and circles are all plane figures.

Look at the picture.

Color all the rectangles blue.

Color all the squares red.

Color all the triangles green.

Color all the circles yellow.

Dot to Dot to Dot

Figures that are the same size and shape are congruent.

These squares are congruent.

Use the space below to draw six sets of congruent figures.

Both Sides the Same

Some things have a line of symmetry. This means they are the same on both sides.

Draw a line through each picture that has a line of symmetry.

5. Look around the room. List two objects that have a line of symmetry.

a. _____

b. _____

Inch by Inch

An inch is a unit you use to measure things.

This inchworm is 1 inch long.

Estimate how long each item is. Then measure the item with a ruler.

1. _____ estimate   _____ inches

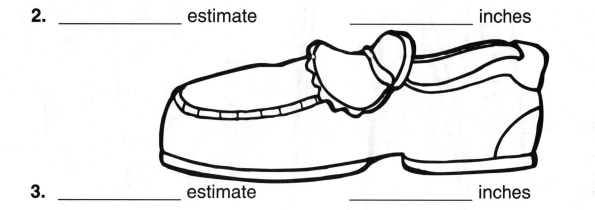

2. _____ estimate   _____ inches

3. _____ estimate   _____ inches

4. _____ estimate   _____ inches

In the space below, draw a rectangle that is about 5 inches long.

Funny Fry Fun

Use a ruler to measure each fry.

Color the 3-inch fries yellow.

Color the 4-inch fries green.

Color the 5-inch fries red.

Color the leftover fries blue.

Tiny Bubbles

You can measure how long things are by using a centimeter ruler.

Use a centimeter ruler.

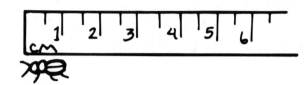

Place your ruler across the center of each bubble.

Measure each bubble.

Write the length inside each bubble.

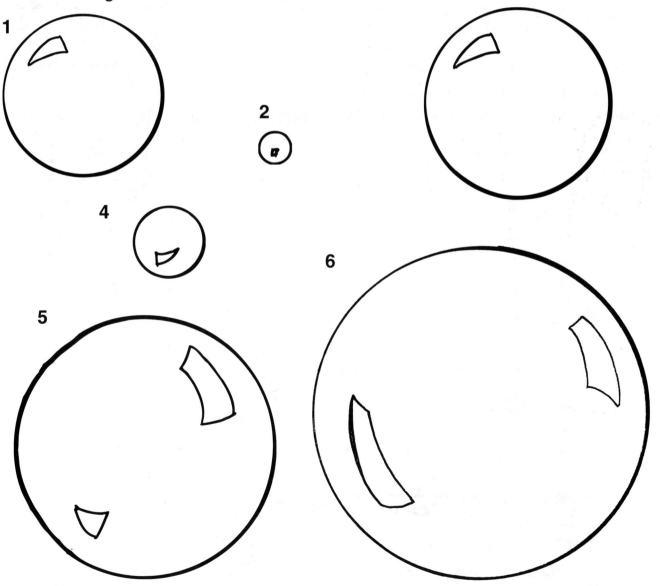

Going Up!

10 centimeters can also be called 1 decimeter.

A decimeter is larger than a centimeter.

List four things that would be about 1 decimeter long.

1. _____

2. _____

3. _____

4. _____

List four things that would be about 2 decimeters long.

5. _____

6. _____

7. _____

8. _____

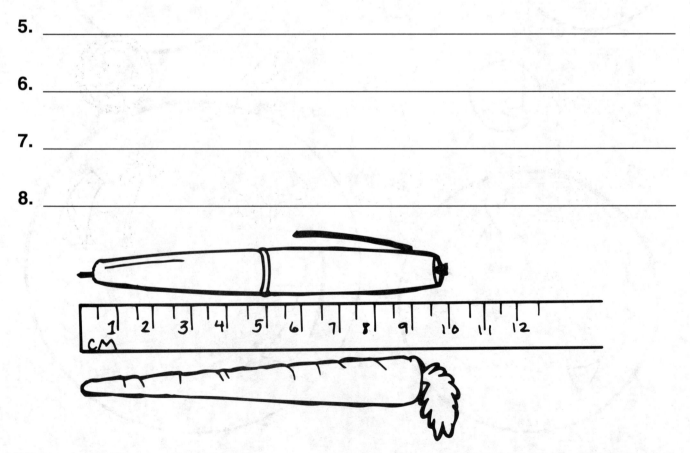

Weighing In

A pound is used to measure how much something weighs.

These things all weigh about 1 pound.

Look at the pictures below.

Color the objects that weigh less than 1 pound yellow.

Color the objects that weigh more than 1 pound green.

Hot Stuff?

A thermometer is used to measure temperature.
A thermometer tells us how hot or cold something is.

 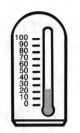

Read each problem.

Color the thermometer red to show the temperature that is given.

1. Bobby is sick. He can't go outside to play because he has a fever of 100°F.

2. Andie is happy because it is snowing outside. She must wear her coat and gloves to play outside. The temperature feels very cold at 30°F.

3. Sandra wants to go swimming. She is glad the day is so hot. It's 90°F, and it's warm enough to swim.

A Fair Share

A fraction is a part of something.

Most things can be divided into smaller or equal parts.

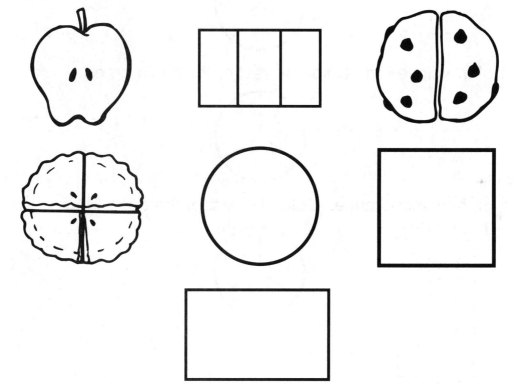

Follow the directions.

1. Draw a circle around the picture that shows the fraction ½.

2. Place an X on the picture that shows the fraction ¼.

3. Divide the circle into two equal parts.

4. Divide the square into four equal parts.

5. Divide the rectangle into two equal parts.

Fun in the Sun

A fraction shows a part of an item.

Some items can be divided into equal parts.

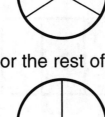

Color the picture to show the fraction.

1. Color $\frac{1}{3}$ of the circle yellow. Color the rest of the circle blue.

2. Color $\frac{1}{3}$ of the circle red. Color the rest of the circle green.

3. Color $\frac{2}{3}$ of the circle orange. Color the rest of the circle blue.

Draw a line to match each picture to the fraction it shows.

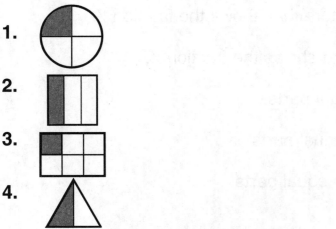

1. $\frac{1}{4}$

2. $\frac{1}{2}$

3. $\frac{1}{3}$

4. $\frac{1}{6}$

A Certain Spot

Everything has a spot where it belongs, and so do numbers!

The number 729 shows that each number has a certain spot.

The 7 is in the hundreds spot.

The 2 is in the tens spot.

And the 9 is in the ones spot.

All together this is the number 729!

Look at the picture.

Circle the numbers in the hundreds spot.

Place an X on the numbers in the tens spot.

Draw a square around the numbers in the ones spot.

Counting Up

Start by putting a circle around the number 1.

Then read across the page, moving from left to right to look for the next number that is greater.

Then circle that number.

When you reach the end of line, move to the next line underneath it.

Continue circling in this manner until you reach 500.

1	7	2	23	20	16
18	12	28	36	19	63
64	14	8	70	100	99
72	150	154	130	82	11
200	185	278	295	300	301
103	343	334	33	384	392
400	420	112	438	483	96
412	490	497	216	48	500

A Little Bit More

Practice writing numbers with hundreds, tens, and ones.

7 hundreds   6 tens   5 ones = 765

	Hundreds	Tens	Ones	
1.	8	6	1	= _____
2.	9	9	9	= _____
3.	7	4	2	= _____
4.	8	1	5	= _____
5.	4	6	7	= _____
6.	6	2	3	= _____

Think About It

If 100 pennies = $ 1.00, then 900 pennies = $ _____.

Big Under the Big Top

Look at each circus picture.

Rearrange the numerals to find the largest new number.

Write the greatest three-digit numeral possible.

Example: 275 → 752

1. ______________________ 3. ______________________

2. ______________________ 4. ______________________

Where Does It Go?

Look at the library books below.

Use the number on the front of the book that is not shelved to decide if the book goes before, between, or after the books that are on the shelf.

Circle the correct answer.

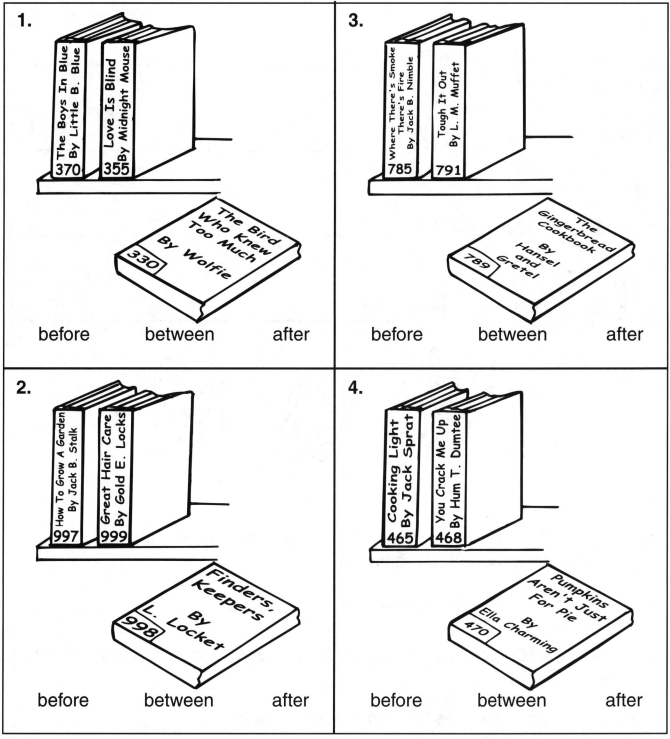

1.

The Boys In Blue By Little B. Blue — 370
Love Is Blind By Midnight Mouse — 355

The Bird Who Knew Too Much By Wolfie — 330

before   between   after

2.

How To Grow A Garden By Jack B. Stalk — 997
Great Hair Care By Gold E. Locks — 999

Finders, Keepers By L. Locket — 998

before   between   after

3.

Where There's Smoke There's Fire By Jack B. Nimble — 785
Tough It Out By L. M. Muffet — 791

The Gingerbread Cookbook By Hansel and Gretel — 789

before   between   after

4.

Cooking Light By Jack Sprat — 465
You Crack Me Up By Hum T. Dumtee — 468

Pumpkins Aren't Just For Pie By Ella Charming — 470

before   between   after

Which Way Do We Go?

Look at the numbers below.

Write them in order from smallest to largest.

1. 459   951   876   _____

2. 976   796   697   _____

3. 456   457   455   _____

4. 600   400   900   _____

5. 215   512   152   _____

Think About It

1. Alicia is 40 years old. Her daughter Chloe is 3 years old. Her other daughter Kayla Beth is 11 years old.

Write their ages from smallest to largest. _____

2. Tristan has 100 pennies. His Uncle Ethan has 450 pennies. Tristan's friend Brett has 400 pennies.

Write the amount of pennies from smallest to largest. _____

Hero Zero

Poor Hero Zero. He's lost all his zeros. Without those zeros, he can't be a hero!

Help return his zeros by circling each correct answer that equals zero.

1. $9 \times 1 = 0$

6. $11 \times 3 = 0$

2. $7 \times 0 = 0$

7. $11 \times 11 = 0$

3. $12 \times 0 = 0$

8. $4 \times 0 = 0$

4. $2 \times 4 = 0$

9. $1 \times 0 = 0$

5. $8 \times 0 = 0$

10. $0 \times 1 = 0$

How many zeros did you find?_____

Draw all the zeros you found on Hero Zero's costume so he can be a hero again! Just for fun, color his costume when you are finished.

Number One

Fill in the blank on each multiplication problem.

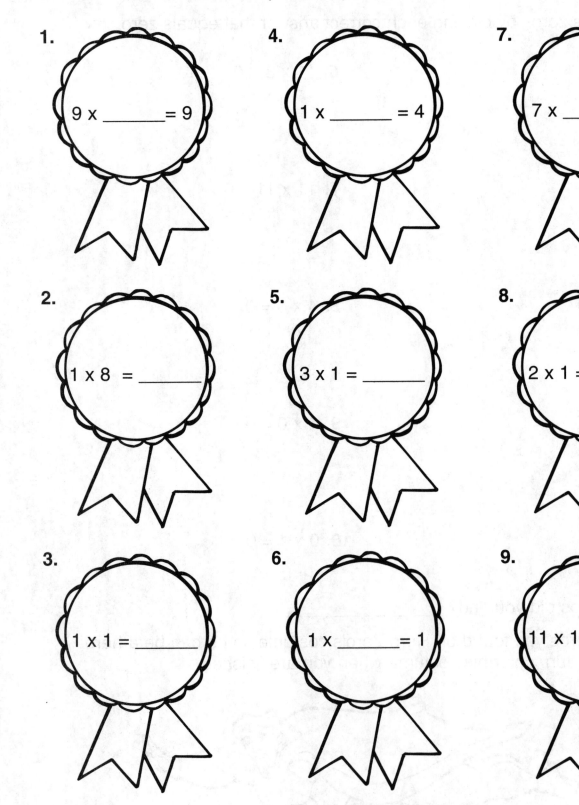

1. 9 x _____ = 9

4. 1 x _____ = 4

7. 7 x _____ = 7

2. 1 x 8 = _____

5. 3 x 1 = _____

8. 2 x 1 = _____

3. 1 x 1 = _____

6. 1 x _____ = 1

9. 11 x 1 = _____

152

Double Time

Answer these multiplication problems as fast as you can!

1. 1 x 2 =

2. 2 x 2 =

3. 3 x 2 =

4. 4 x 2 =

5. 5 x 2 =

6. 6 x 2 =

7. 7 x 2 =

8. 8 x 2 =

9. 9 x 2 =

10. 10 x 2 =

11. 11 x 2 =

12. 12 x 2 =

What's Hidden?

Practice multiplying by three.

Color only the boxes that have a correct answer.

4 x 3 = 11	4 x 3 = 12	3 x 1 = 3	3 x 9 = 27	3 x 8 = 29	3 x 2 = 9
3 x 1 = 0	3 x 4 = 9	3 x 2 = 0	3 x 1 = 3	3 x 11 = 11	3 x 12 = 33
2 x 3 = 18	3 x 8 = 24	3 x 12 = 36	7 x 3 = 21	6 x 3 = 12	3 x 1 =4
9 x 3 = 17	3 x 0 = 3	2 x 3 = 8	3 x 9 = 27	3 x 10 = 40	7 x 3 = 29
3 x 3 = 11	3 x 6 = 18	3 x 2 = 6	7 x 3 = 21	3 x 6 = 36	3 x 1 = 6
3 x 0 = 30	5 x 3 = 14	3 x 7 = 24	9 x 3 = 17	3 x 4 = 7	6 x 3 = 9

Four Square

Answer each problem.

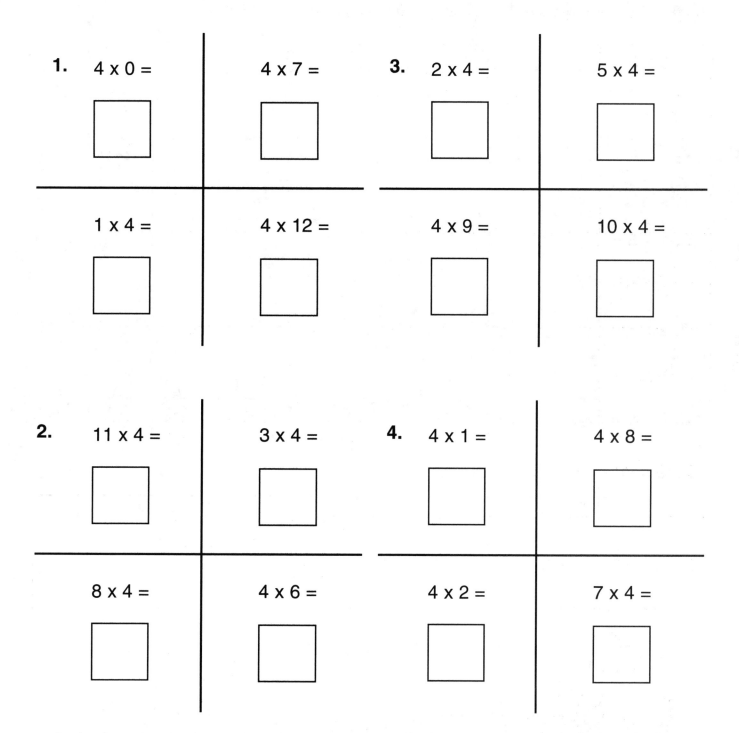

1. 4 x 0 = ☐   4 x 7 = ☐   **3.** 2 x 4 = ☐   5 x 4 = ☐

1 x 4 = ☐   4 x 12 = ☐   4 x 9 = ☐   10 x 4 = ☐

2. 11 x 4 = ☐   3 x 4 = ☐   **4.** 4 x 1 = ☐   4 x 8 = ☐

8 x 4 = ☐   4 x 6 = ☐   4 x 2 = ☐   7 x 4 = ☐

Star Light, Star Bright

Find the answer to each multiplication problem.

Use the five points on each star to help you find the answer.

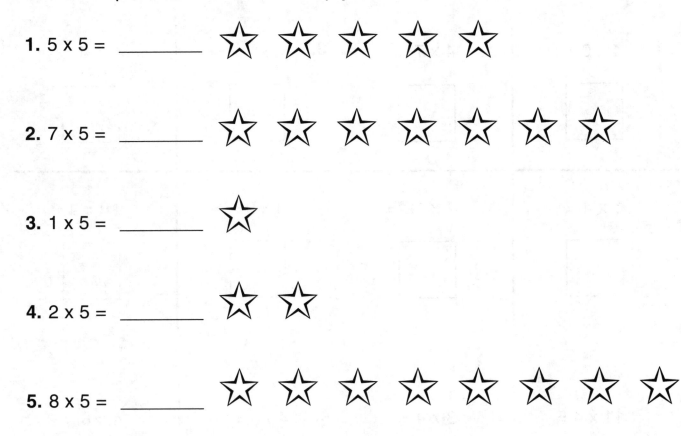

1. 5 x 5 = _____ ☆ ☆ ☆ ☆ ☆

2. 7 x 5 = _____ ☆ ☆ ☆ ☆ ☆ ☆ ☆

3. 1 x 5 = _____ ☆

4. 2 x 5 = _____ ☆ ☆

5. 8 x 5 = _____ ☆ ☆ ☆ ☆ ☆ ☆ ☆ ☆

In the space below, draw 10 stars.

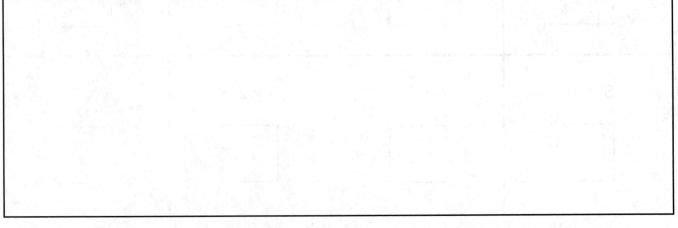

How many total points are on the 10 stars? Write an equation to help you find the answer.

_____ X _____ = _____

Mixed Multiplication

Read and solve each problem.

1. Crede has two dogs, Kahntu and Princess. Each dog has one dog collar. How many collars are there in all?

_____ x _____ = _____

2. Tommy, Bobby, and James all want to ride the bumper cars. Each person needs three tickets to ride the cars. How many tickets in all do they need?

_____ x _____ = _____

3. There are five giant spiders spinning their webs. Each giant spider has eight giant legs. How many giant spider legs are there in all?

_____ x _____ = _____

4. Kristen, Allison, Shea, and Derek all had cookies for their snack. Each person ate four cookies. How many cookies were eaten in all?

_____ x _____ = _____

Know Your Multiplication

Remember that multiplication is another way to add numbers.

The answer to an addition problem is the sum.

The answer to a multiplication problem is the product.

Look at the pictures.

Write the sum for each problem. Then write the product.

1.

2 cats + 2 cats + 2 cats = _____ cats　　　　　　2 x 3 = _____

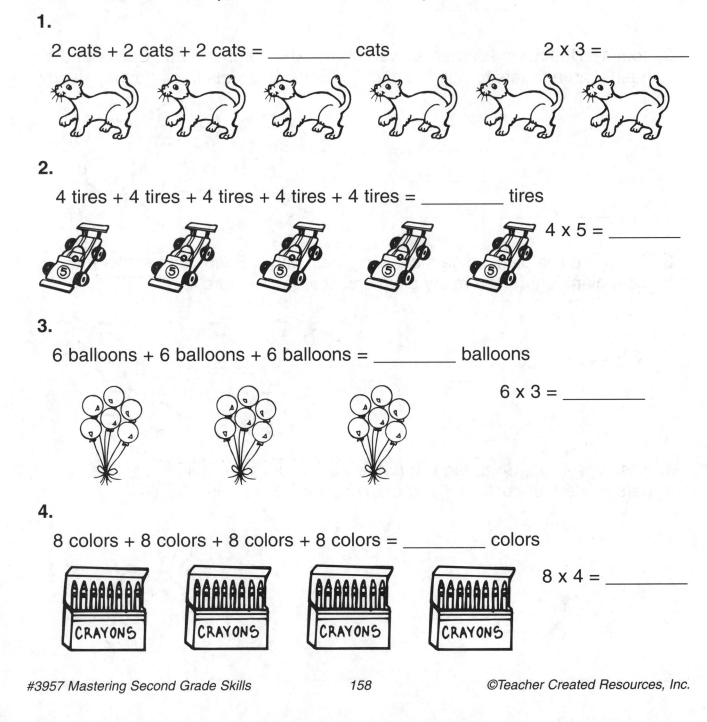

2.

4 tires + 4 tires + 4 tires + 4 tires + 4 tires = _____ tires

4 x 5 = _____

3.

6 balloons + 6 balloons + 6 balloons = _____ balloons

6 x 3 = _____

4.

8 colors + 8 colors + 8 colors + 8 colors = _____ colors

8 x 4 = _____

CRAYONS　CRAYONS　CRAYONS　CRAYONS

Putting It All Together

Answer the multiplication problems.

1 x 11 = _____

3 x 7 = _____

0 x 9 = _____

2 x 8 = _____

4 x 12 = _____

5 x 5 = _____

Oops! The pickle fell off the bun. Answer this final problem!

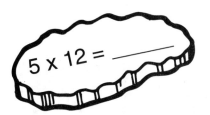

5 x 12 = _____

Being a Good Citizen

A good citizen cares about others. A good citizen makes the community a better place to live.

Circle each thing a good citizen might do.

1. vote in elections

2. obey laws

3. throw trash on the ground

4. learn more about the government

5. be patriotic

RECYCLE

Match each word to the correct meaning.

6. Government   **A.** a choice that is counted

7. Judge   **B.** a group of people who make the rules and laws

8. Vote   **C.** the person who is the leader in court

9. Freedom   **D.** giving people the right to make decisions

You and Your Community

You are a citizen of your community. Your school is a community. You are a citizen of your school and even your class.

Imagine you had $100 that you could give to your class. What could the class do with the money that would help the most people?

1. _____

2. _____

3. _____

4. _____

What are three qualities a good citizen should have? In other words, what type of person should he or she be?

1. _____

2. _____

3. _____

She's a Grand Flag

Color the flag.

Start with the first stripe. Color it and every other stripe red. Leave the other stripes white.

Color the square blue and leave the stars white.

Fun Flag Facts

1. The American flag has _____ stars.

2. The 50 stars represent the 50 _____ . California, Utah, Maine, and Tennessee are some of the 50 states.

3. The _____ stripes represent the original 13 colonies.

4. The first flag was sewn by a woman named _____ .

5. This flag is the flag of the United _____ of _____ .

Every Vote Counts

Mrs. Castleberry's class is having a reward party.

Her students must decide on a pizza party or an ice cream party.

The students voted on which party to have by circling their choice.

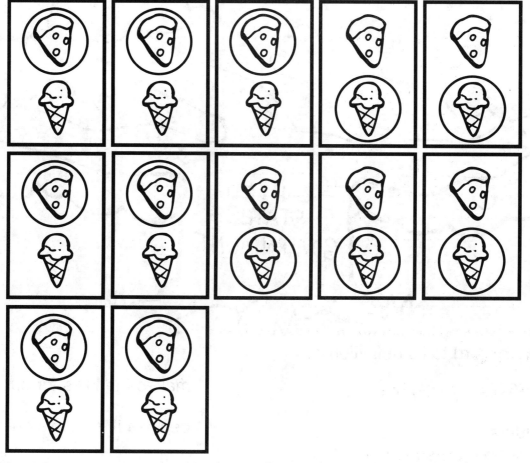

Look at the children's votes in Mrs. Castleberry's class. Answer the questions.

1. How many children voted for ice cream? _____

2. How many children voted for pizza? _____

3. Why is every vote important? _____

4. What kind of party will the children have? _____

5. How do you know which party the children will have? _____

Branching Out

Identify the three branches of the United States government. The three branches are the judicial branch, the executive branch, and the legislative branch. Write the name of each branch of government on a tree branch.

Match each word to its definition.

4. President   makes the laws for our country

5. Congress   decides if the laws are fair

6. Supreme Court   has three branches

7. Government   leads our country

Just for Fun

If you could be president, what three things would you try to do for your country?

1. _____

2. _____

3. _____

Rights and Freedoms

Citizens of the United States have certain freedoms that are listed in the Bill of Rights.

The Bill of Rights is part of the United States' Constitution. It lists the freedoms that Americans have.

1. What does the word freedom mean to you?

_____

What are some freedoms you have at school?

2. _____

3. _____

4. _____

What is one freedom you do not have that you wish you did have?

5. _____

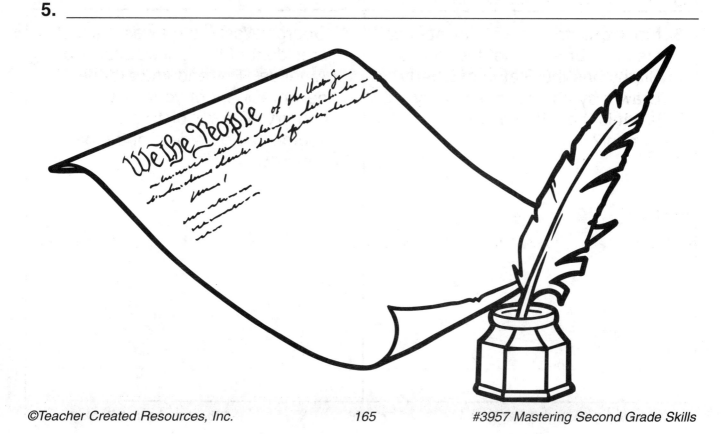

This Land Is Your Land

A country is a certain area of land.

Look at each square. Read and follow each direction.

1. Imagine you could name a new country. What would you name this new country? Draw a picture of the country.	**2.** Every country has a flag. A country's flag tells something about the country. The United States' flag has 50 stars because there are 50 states. Draw and color the new country's flag. Write one thing that is special about the flag.
3. Many countries have a symbol or statue. For example, the United States has the Statue of Liberty. Draw a symbol for the country. What is the name of your symbol?	**4.** George Washington was the first president of the United States of America. Pretend you are the new president of your new country. Draw a picture of yourself as president of the new country.

Making Your Own Rules

A good citizen helps the community.

A school is a type of community. Everyone in the school works together. Everyone is there to help each other.

Look at the school rules listed below.

Which rules help the community?

Which rules are not helpful to the school?

Circle the rules that are good for the school community.

Write an X on the rules that are not good for the school community.

1. Throw food in the cafeteria.

3. Never open a book.

5. Eat a good lunch.

2. Be quiet in the halls.

4. Be involved and answer questions.

6. Smile and be happy.

Our School Community

Your school is a community.

Look at each picture below.

On the lines provided, tell how each person helps or contributes to the school community.

1. Principal

_____

_____

4. Student

_____

_____

2. Teacher

_____

_____

5. Cafeteria Worker

_____

_____

3. Volunteer

_____

_____

6. Librarian

_____

_____

Everyone Works Together

In a community, everyone works together to make the community a good place.

Many families live in neighborhoods. Neighborhoods are small communities.

Draw a picture to represent each person listed.

Underneath the picture list one thing he or she does to help the community.

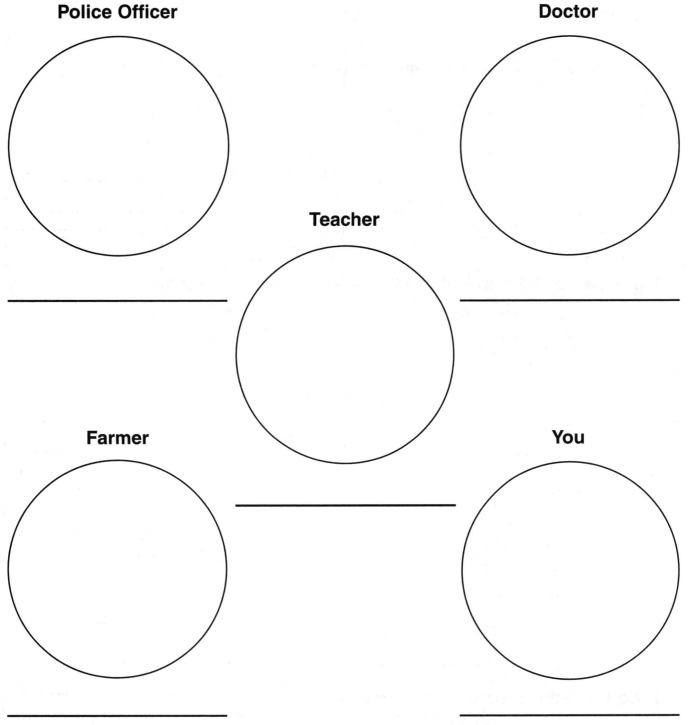

Police Officer

Doctor

Teacher

Farmer

You

Mapping Your Neighborhood

Use the word bank to answer the questions.

map key	symbol	directions
compass rose	map title	location

1. A picture that stands for something on a map is a _____ .

2. A _____ explains the symbols on a map.

3. The part of the map that shows the directions north, south, east, and west is

the _____ .

4. The _____ is like the title of a book. It tells what the

map is about.

5. People use a map to find the _____ of a place.

6. North, south, east, and west are all _____ on a map.

170

Think About It

A community needs many kinds of people.

Think about how each person is needed in a community. Then answer the questions.

1. Why does a community need a police officer?

_____

_____

2. Why might a community need a grocery store owner?

_____

_____

3. Why would a community need a mayor?

_____

_____

4. Why would a community need a doctor?

_____

_____

People That Help Us

Many people in our communities are there to help us.

Look at the pictures below.

List ways these people in your community can help you.

1. _____   1. _____

2. _____   2. _____

1. _____   1. _____

2. _____   2. _____

House Hunting

A neighborhood is a place where people live.

Draw your dream house in the neighborhood below. When you are done, write the name the street on the street sign.

Where in the World Am I?

Bobby forgot to label his vacation pictures. See if you can help him remember where he was. Use the words in the box.

desert	forest	mountain
ocean	island	

1. _____

2. _____

3. _____

4. _____

5. _____

Mix and Match

Draw a line to match each object to its place.

1.    desert

2.    neighborhood

3.   farm

4.   ocean

5.   city

6.    river

Two Colorful Continents

Look at the map.

Label and color each continent.

1. Color North America blue.

2. Color South America red.

3. Draw a star on the continent where the United States is located.

4. Draw a smiley face on the continent that is south of North America.

5. If you live on one of the two continents, draw a house on that continent.

Words to Know

Choose a word from the word bank that fits each clue. Write the answer on the correct line. Then use the letters in each box to find the mystery words.

oceans	geography	continents
globe	resource	equator
conservation	island	

1. a model of our planet Earth _____

2. an imaginary line that divides Earth in half _____

3. something we use that comes from Earth _____

4. the largest bodies of water on Earth _____

5. land with water all around it _____

6. saving our Earth's resources _____

7. the largest bodies of land _____

8. the study of Earth _____

1. R	**5.** E
2. A	**6.** U
3. O	**7.** T
4. R	**8.** H

Mystery words: ___ ___ ___   ___ ___ ___ ___ ___
                     3   6   4   5   2   1   7   8

Land and Water

There are seven continents. Can you name them?

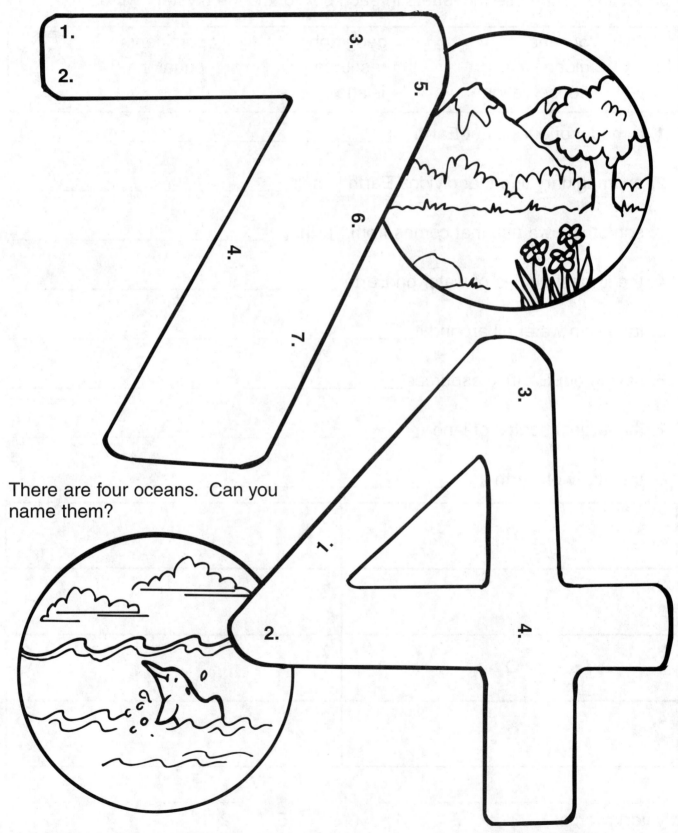

1.

2.

3.

5.

4.

6.

7.

There are four oceans. Can you name them?

1.

2.

3.

4.

Understanding Time

Look at each picture.

If the picture shows something that happened in the past, write the word past underneath the picture.

If the picture shows something that happened in the present, write the word present underneath the picture.

1. _____

2. _____

3. _____

4. _____

The Making of Things

Inventions are new ideas that are made into things. The telephone, computer, and television are examples of inventions that are useful.

Imagine you are an inventor.

Think about the hours you spend at school.

What is something you could invent that would make your day at school even better?

1. The name of my invention is:

_____

2. What my invention does:

_____

3. What did I use to make my invention?

_____

4. Do you think other people will like your invention? Why or why not?

_____

5. Draw and color a picture of your invention here.

Getting Time in a Line

A timeline puts things in the order in which they happened.

History has a timeline, and so do you. From the minute you were born, your timeline began.

Look at the timeline below.

Write each answer on the correct line.

Draw pictures for your timeline.

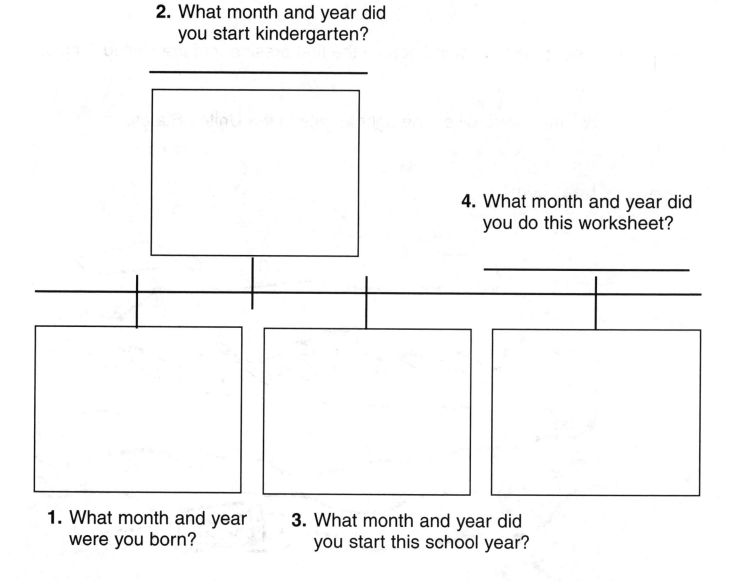

2. What month and year did you start kindergarten?

4. What month and year did you do this worksheet?

1. What month and year were you born?

3. What month and year did you start this school year?

Time in a Bottle

Number the events in history.

Start with #1 to show which event happened first.

_____ Man landed on the moon.

_____ Columbus discovered America.

_____ George Washington became the first president of the United States.

_____ Women were given the right to vote in the United States.

_____ I was born.

Important Words

Match each word to the correct definition.

1. history   a place where people live

2. landmark   a well-known object at a certain place

3. settler   the story of the past

4. shelter   a place ruled by another country

5. colony   a person who makes his or her home in a new place

Celebrate!

There are many special holidays to celebrate. Many of these holidays have their own special symbols.

Independence Day is best known for its fireworks. Christmas is known for its festive Christmas trees. Valentine's Day is known for its red hearts.

Imagine you could create your own holiday to celebrate you.

Write a brief story telling all about your new holiday. What special colors would you use? What special symbols would you have?

Graph It!

A bar graph is a graph that shows how many of a certain thing there is.

Look at the bar graph below.

Then answer the questions.

Brothers and Sisters					
Shelly					
Amanda	▨	▨			
Mark	▨	▨	▨		
Robert	▨				
Rhonda	▨	▨	▨	▨	

1. Who has the most brothers and sisters? _____

2. Who has more brothers and sisters than Mark? _____

3. Who has no brothers or sisters? _____

4. Who has only one brother or sister? _____

Around the World

The globe below is empty! Someone has erased the pictures of the world.
Draw an outline of the continent where you live on the empty globe below.

When you are finished drawing the outline,

1. Write the name of the continent where you live.

2. Color the land on your continent green.

3. Color the water around your continent blue.

4. Label the oceans that are on each side of your continent.

5. Draw a star on your continent to show where you live.

The Key Concept

A map key shows you how to read a map. A map key shows all of the map symbols and tells what each symbol means.

Look at the map key below.

On the line, write the name of your city.

Draw a symbol for each item listed. The first one has been done for you.

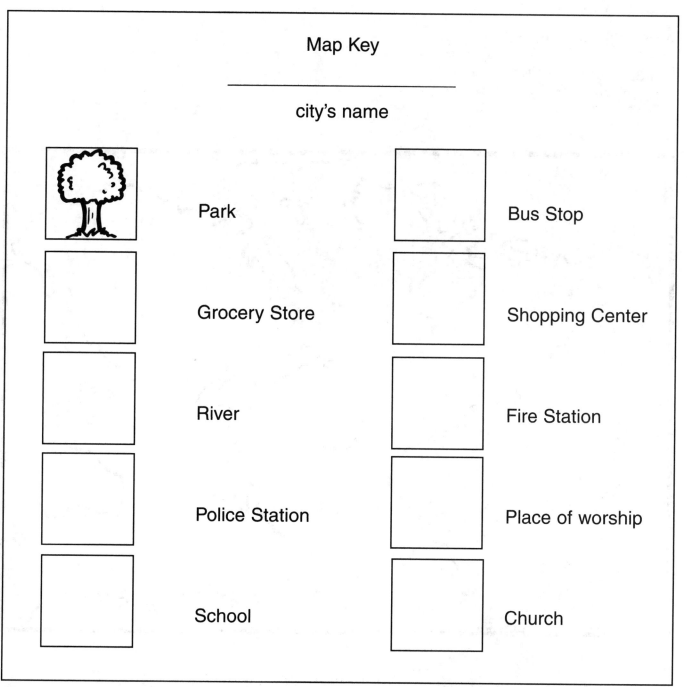

Map Key

_____

city's name

Park

Grocery Store

River

Police Station

School

Bus Stop

Shopping Center

Fire Station

Place of worship

Church

Do You See What I "Sea"?

There are seven continents in our world.

There are also four major oceans. Use a map to find out what they are.

Look at the map below. Find where each ocean should be.

Write on the map the name of each ocean in the color listed below.

Pacific Ocean—green

Atlantic Ocean—red

Arctic Ocean—black

Indian Ocean—blue

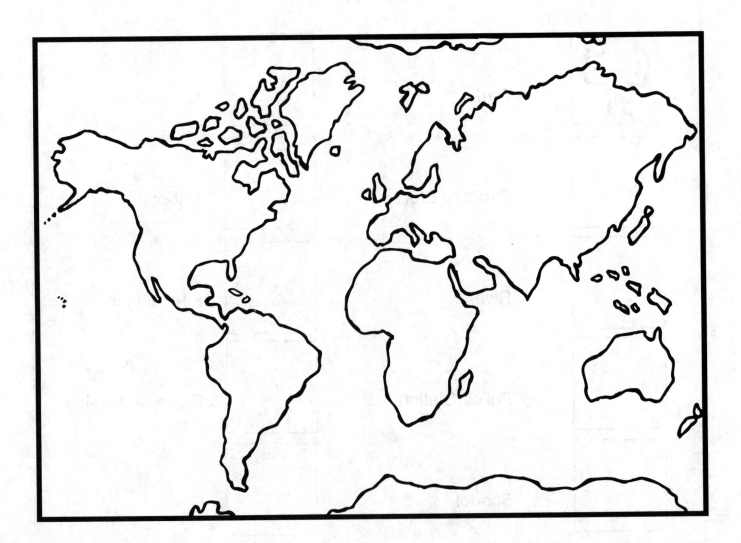

The United States

Below is an outline map of the United States.

1. Find the area of the map where your state would be. Draw an outline of your state and color it yellow.

2. Write the name of your state underneath the outline.

3. Find the state that is a group of islands. Write the name underneath the islands. Color this state red.

4. Find the area on the map where Florida and California would be. Write a "F" where Florida should be. Write a "C" where California should be.

5. Find the outline of Alaska. Color this state purple.

Can you name the states that border or touch the state where you live?

List the names of these states: _____

_____

_____

List the names of these states:

Mapping Your Own Place

Maps are guides to help you find your way.

Maps can be of places we know well or places we've never been to.

In the space below, draw a map of your classroom.

Use the map key to help you with your picture.

Classroom Map Key

a	Student's Desk	**d**	Chalkboard
b	Teacher's Desk	**e**	Door
c	Window	**f**	Bulletin Board

Alive or Not?

Draw a circle around four objects that are living objects.

Draw an X on four objects that are not living.

What You Know

Read each statement about plants and decide if it is true or false.

Write the letter *T* beside each true statement.

Write the letter *F* beside each false statement.

_____**1.** Plants grow from seeds.

_____**2.** All plants need lots of water.

_____**3.** Plants can get water from rain.

_____**4.** Sunlight helps plants grow.

_____**5.** Some plants produce food you can eat.

_____**6.** The roots on a plant are not very important.

In the space below, draw a picture of a plant you've seen near your home or school.

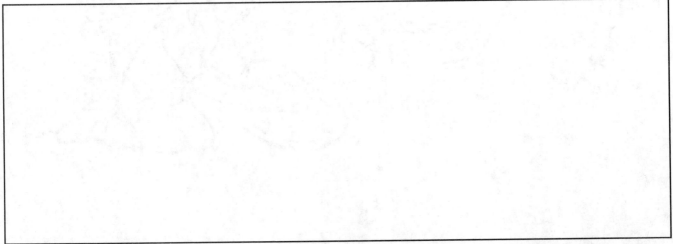

What Happens First?

Look at the pictures.

Number the pictures from 1–6 in the order they should go.

Flower Power

Look at the word in the center of each flower.

Write a fact about that group of living things on each petal.

1.   **2.**

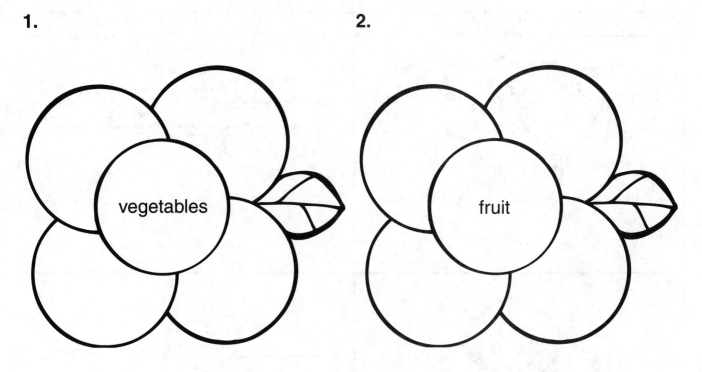

3.   **4.**

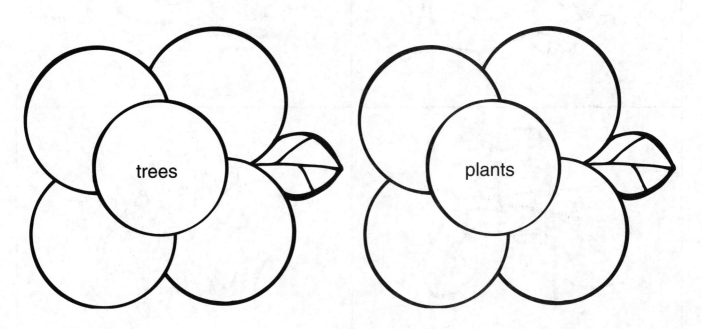

It's All About the Parts

All things are made of parts.

Label each part of the plant below.

Use the word bank if you need help.

seeds	flower	leaves
stem	roots	pollen

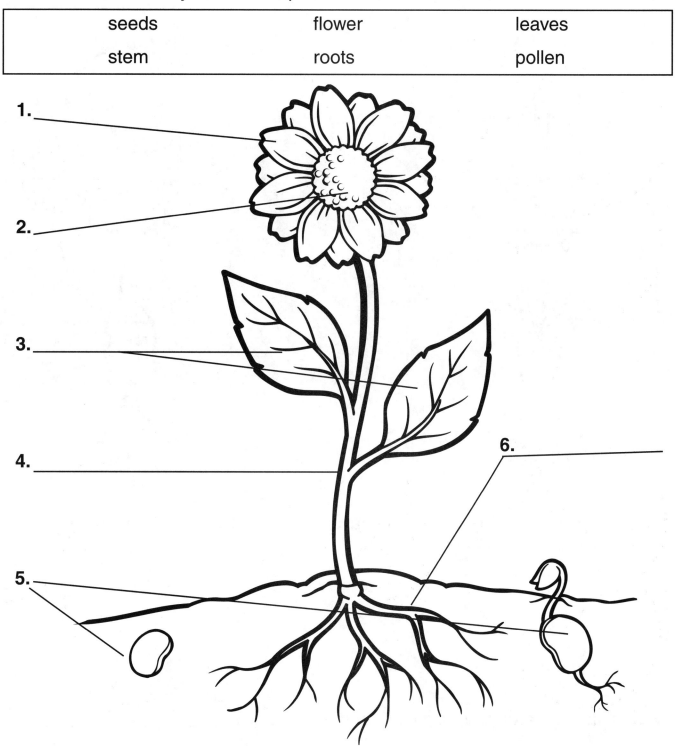

1. _____

2. _____

3. _____

4. _____

5. _____

6. _____

The Daily Plant

People use plants every day.

Look at the pictures below.

Then draw a line to match each plant to the way it is used.

1.

2.

3.

4.

Imagine you are a scientist and you have just created a new plant. In the space below, draw a picture of your new plant.

What is the name of your new plant and how is it used? _____

_____

All Kinds of Animals

Scientists divide animals into four groups. These four groups are mammals, amphibians, reptiles, and birds.

Look at the four squares below.

Then write the name of one other animal in each group.

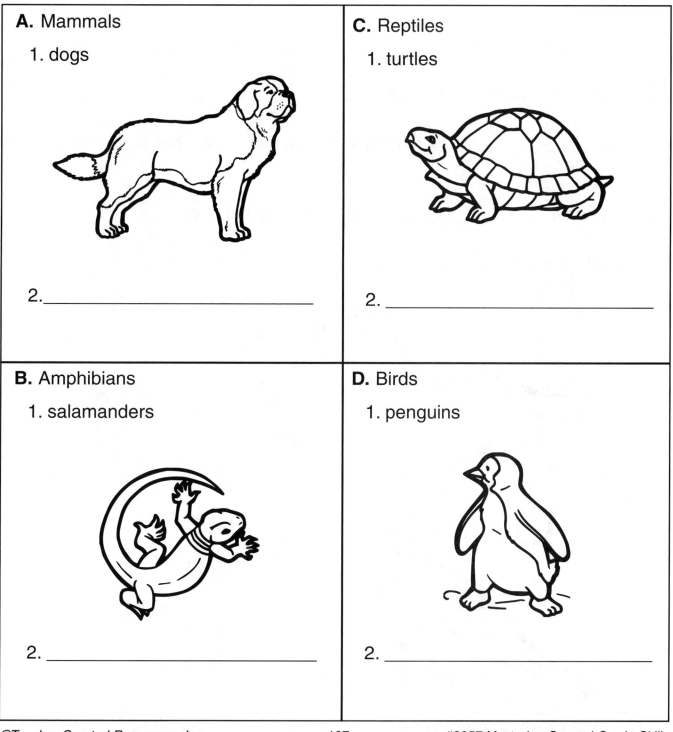

A. Mammals

    1. dogs

2._____

C. Reptiles

    1. turtles

2. _____

B. Amphibians

    1. salamanders

2. _____

D. Birds

    1. penguins

2. _____

Learning More About Animals

Use the word bank to help you answer the questions.

mammals	air	feathers
frogs	eggs	insects

1. All mammals need to breathe _____ to survive.

2. Mammals do not lay _____ , but birds do.

3. Animals that have six legs are _____.

4. _____ are amphibians because they live both in and out of the water.

5. Birds have _____ , but mammals do not.

6. People are _____.

Creepy Crawlies

Insects are everywhere!

Insects are amazing because their bodies are not made of bones. Most insects have a hard outer shell to protect their bodies.

Insects' bodies are made of three main parts: the head, the thorax, and the abdomen. They are different from spiders because they have only six legs, not eight like their spider friends.

Look at the picture of the insect.

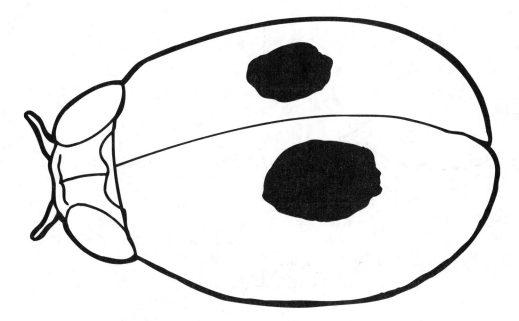

Then fill in the blanks and follow any directions given.

1. Use a black crayon and draw _____ legs on the insect.

2. The three parts of the insect's body are the _____ ,
_____ , and _____ .

3. On what part of the body are an insect's eyes? _____

4. Does the spider or the insect have more legs? _____

5. Think of where you live. List two places you have seen insects.

_____   _____

Insects Can Be Beautiful

Some insects change the way they look.

In the boxes below, draw each stage of the butterfly as it changes from an egg to an adult.

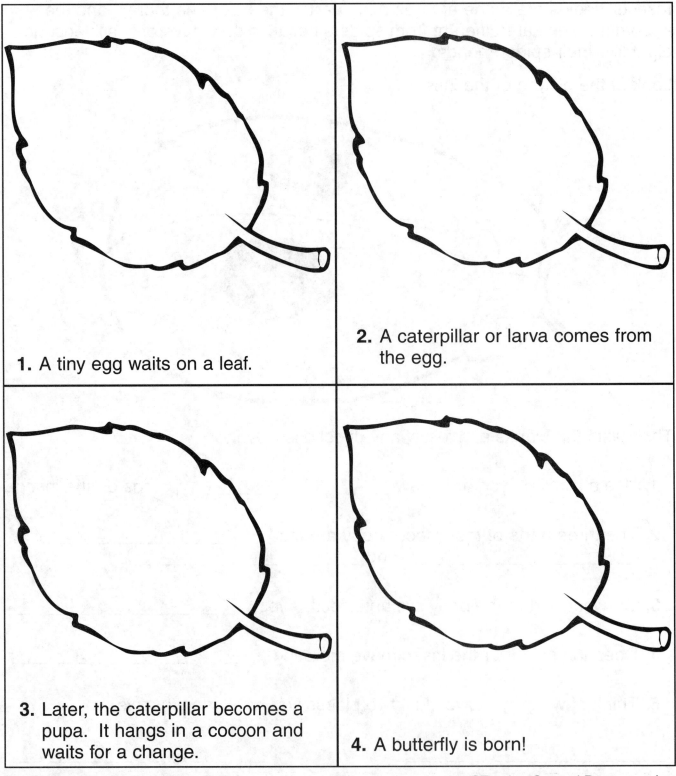

1. A tiny egg waits on a leaf.

2. A caterpillar or larva comes from the egg.

3. Later, the caterpillar becomes a pupa. It hangs in a cocoon and waits for a change.

4. A butterfly is born!

From Baby to Adult

All animals start as babies. Then they become adults.

Read the name of each baby animal.

Next write the name of the adult animal that it becomes.

1. puppy _____

2. fawn _____

3. calf _____

4. colt _____

5. kitten _____

6. chick_____

Now draw a picture of your favorite animal as a baby and as an adult.

My favorite animal is called a/an _____ When it is

a baby. It is called a/an _____ when it becomes

an adult.

Catch Me If You Can!

Animals that are being hunted by another animal are prey.

Animals that are the hunters are predators.

Look at each picture.

Decide if the animal is usually a predator or the prey.

Write your answer on the line.

1. _____

2. _____

3. _____

4. _____

Following the Food Chain

5. A frog eats an insect.

Then a _____ eats the frog.

6. A fish eats a frog.

Then a _____ eats the fish.

Do you like to eat fish? _____

Animal Habitats

Animals live in habitats that are special for them.

Match each animal to its habitat.

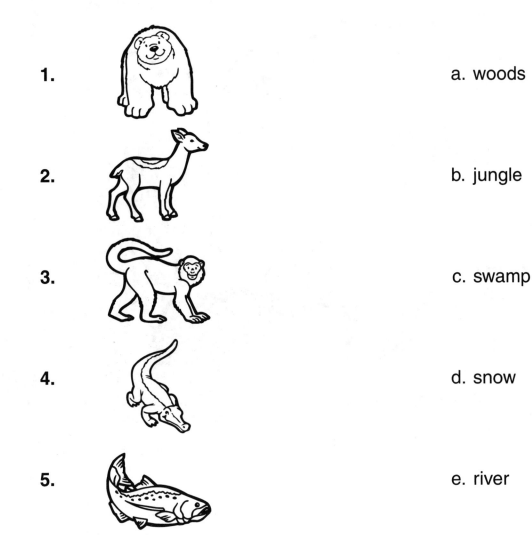

1.   a. woods

2.   b. jungle

3.   c. swamp

4.   d. snow

5.   e. river

Draw a picture of a turtle in its natural habitat.

Reading a Weather Map

Use the weather map to help you answer the questions.

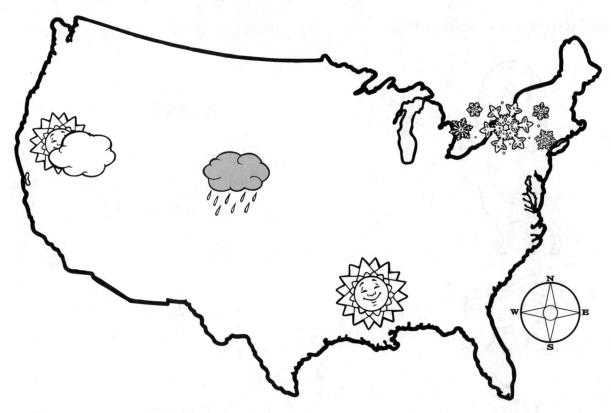

1. What is the weather like in the South?

_____

2. Do the people in the North need their coats and gloves today?

_____

3. What type of weather are the people in California having?

_____

4. In which area is it most likely to rain?

_____

The Weather Around You

Look at each picture.

First, describe the weather in the picture.

Then, write what season it is.

1. _____

2. _____

1. _____

2. _____

1. _____

2. _____

1. _____

2. _____

Hot or Not?

A thermometer is used to measure the temperature. Liquid in a thermometer rises or falls to show us how hot or cold it is.

When a thermometer reads 32°F water can freeze. This is the temperature that produces snow!

Read each thermometer.

Write the temperature on the line.

Daily High Temperatures

Sunday   Monday   Tuesday   Wednesday   Thursday   Friday   Saturday

_____ _____ _____ _____ _____ _____ _____

1. Which day had the lowest temperature? _____

2. Which day had the highest temperature? _____

3. Which days had the same temperature? _____

4. Which day was cold enough for snow? _____

5. What was the temperature on Wednesday? _____

The Water Cycle

Earth's water goes in an endless cycle.

Look at the words in the clouds, and then place each word where it belongs on the water cycle.

1. _____

2. _____

3. _____

Unscramble It

Unscramble each group of letters to find a weather-related word.

1. nria _____

5. smort _____

2. tslee _____

6. darzzlib _____

3. obwnair _____

7. odtorna _____

4. owsn _____

8. caenihurr _____

Now make a scrambled weather word of your own. See if a friend can unscramble it.

Scrambled Letters: _____

Answer: _____

Sky Surprise

Clouds are always surprising you. If you watch a cloud, it will change shapes. Sometimes you may just see a cloud. Sometimes you may see a special shape if you look at a cloud long enough.

Look at the clouds below and write what shape you see.

Cloud 1: _____

Cloud 3: _____

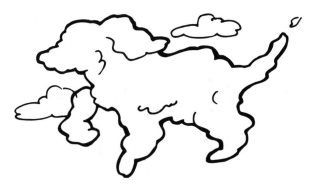

Cloud 2: _____

Cloud 4: _____

Look at the clouds.

Write the name of the type of cloud above each picture.

_____ _____ _____ _____

Use the word bank to help you.

cirrus	stratus	cumulus	nimbus

Long, Long Ago

Fossils are clues to what life was like long ago.
Fossils can be found in ice, rock, tar, or amber.

Read each clue.

Then draw a picture to show what each fossil might look like.

1. a paw print

3. a leaf

2. a dinosaur

4. an insect

Long Gone

Some animals become extinct. If an animal becomes extinct, it means no more of its kind exists anywhere on earth.

1. List two reasons why an animal might become extinct.

_____

_____

2. List two animals that are extinct.

_____

_____

3. List two things people can do to help animals not to become extinct.

_____

_____

4. An animal that is not _____ , but is in danger of becoming extinct, is called an endangered animal.

5. What do you think the world would be like if dinosaurs were not extinct?

_____

_____

_____

Day and Night

Read the paragraph and then answer the questions below.

The planet Earth rotates or spins on its axis. This spinning motion is always in the same direction. It takes 24 hours or one day for Earth to make a complete rotation. Earth's rotation is also what causes day and night. When a part of Earth is facing the sun, it is day. When a part of Earth is away from the sun, it is night. Because Earth moves, it appears that the sun is moving across the sky. However, the sun does not move, rise, or set like we say it does. All of this is caused by Earth's movement and not the sun's.

Read each sentence.

Circle the answer in parentheses that is correct.

1. Earth (falls, spins) like a top.

2. Earth spins in (different directions, the same direction).

3. The sun (moves, does not move) across the sky.

4. As Earth spins or rotates, it becomes (crooked, day or night).

5. When Earth faces the sun, it is (day, night).

6. It takes (72, 24) hours for Earth to complete a rotation.

7. There are (24, 48) hours in a day.

8. The sun is a (planet, star).

The Man in the Moon

There is really no man in the moon. The "face" you sometimes see when you look at the moon is really the moon's craters. The moon is bright enough to see because the sun shines on the moon.

Pretend there really is a man in the moon. What do you think he does all day? What do you think he sees from way out in space? How do you think he got on the moon? What is his name? Now write a story about him in the space below.

_____

_____

_____

_____

_____

_____

_____

_____

_____

The Answers to the Universe

Read the following paragraph. Then circle the correct answer for each question.

Our Solar System has nine named planets. The entire system is made up of the nine planets, their moons, and the sun. The sun is not a planet or a moon. It is actually a star. Our planet Earth is the third planet from the sun. When you look at the sky at night, you may be able to see the moon, depending on what phase the moon is in. If the moon is full, it is easy to spot because it is like a giant ball in the sky. Our moon does not rise and set as it seems, but stays the same in the sky. It is the rotation of Earth that causes both the moon and the sun to "appear" and "disappear" each day.

1. Our Solar System has_____.

    a. 11 planets

    b. 12 planets

    c. 9 named planets

    d. 1 planet

2. The sun, the nine planets, and their moons all make our _____.

    a. solar system

    b. habitat

    c. orbit

    d. Earth

3. When the moon looks like a round ball, it is called _____.

    a. a planet

    b. a golf moon

    c. a pizza

    d. a full moon

4. The moon looks like it rises and sets because_____.

    a. the moon moves

    b. Earth moves

    c. the sun moves

    d. nothing moves

Know Your Stuff

Mary's violet eyes made John stay up nights. Period.

The sentence you just read is a way to help you learn the nine named planets in our solar system.

The first letter of each word stands for a planet:

Mercury, Venus, Earth, Mars, Jupiter, Saturn, Uranus, Neptune, Pluto.

Create two sentences of your own to help remember the nine named planets.

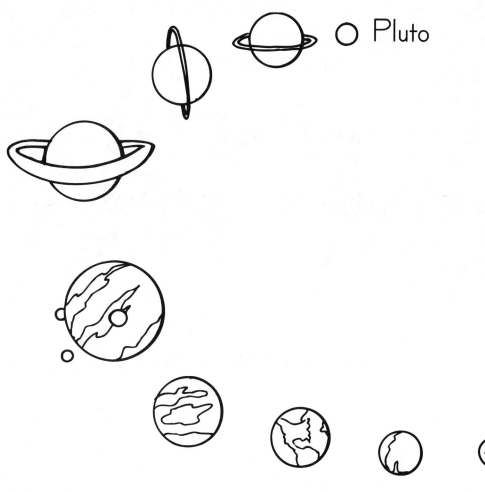

Hint: Your first word must start with the letter *m* and your last word should start with the letter *p*.

1. _____

2. _____

Label each of the nine named planets above. The first one is done for you.

What's a Matter?

All things are made of matter. Matter can be a solid, liquid, or gas.

Look at each picture. Circle the correct state of matter.

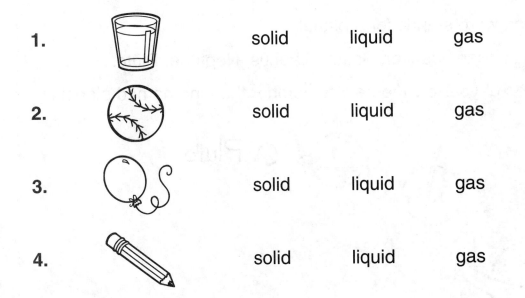

1.   solid   liquid   gas

2.   solid   liquid   gas

3.   solid   liquid   gas

4.   solid   liquid   gas

5. In the space below, draw an example of matter in a solid state.

More That Matters

Find each science word in the word search below. Words may be listed down or across.

```
X  I  M  N  J  N  F  A  O  X  G  Q  X  U  I
C  H  A  N  G  E  L  E  O  V  Q  U  D  K  R
X  E  T  Y  B  P  R  O  P  E  R  T  Y  V  Q
G  S  T  C  M  A  S  S  C  O  D  D  E  T  Q
Z  A  E  L  B  A  D  E  N  S  H  A  P  E  W
A  B  R  S  T  R  O  Q  P  N  M  S  C  I  M
Q  L  Y  L  P  G  P  O  F  E  J  C  Q  R  M
J  Q  I  N  S  O  L  I  D  C  H  K  V  G  Z
A  G  U  D  G  R  A  U  V  P  O  K  A  G  K
F  M  C  G  U  O  B  W  O  N  G  L  P  R  Q
E  G  A  S  G  I  E  M  L  T  O  E  O  H  K
J  N  H  R  Z  Q  D  D  U  G  M  D  R  U  G
T  L  I  Q  U  I  D  W  M  M  B  F  J  Q  I
M  N  M  Z  A  N  T  O  E  D  B  P  W  N  P
E  X  M  U  O  D  T  H  L  O  M  L  A  Z  F
```

solid	gas	volume
mass	solid	change
shape	matter	
vapor	property	

Moving and Changing

A push or pull makes something move. This movement is called force. The force that holds things on Earth is called gravity.

Imagine that something has gone terribly wrong with your classroom. Imagine there is no gravity to hold things down.

In the space below, draw a picture of a day at school with no gravity.

What's Happening?

Look at each picture. Write the word *push* if the object is being pushed. Write *pull* if the object is being pulled.

1. _____

2. _____

3. _____

4. _____

Simple Simon

Simple Simon needs help.

He has a very heavy box that he needs to move.

Help Simple Simon by finding and circling the simple machine that can help him move the heavy box.

Simple Simon needs your help again.

Now that he's moved his box, he needs a tool to open it.

Help Simple Simon by circling the tool that can help him open his box.

More Simple Machines

A simple machine with a slanted surface is a ramp. A ramp is a simple machine that can help you move things.

1. List three ways to use a ramp.

_____

_____

_____

2. How could a ramp be helpful for a person in a wheelchair?

_____

_____

_____

3. How could someone riding a skateboard use a ramp?

_____

_____

_____

4. Are there any ramps at your school? If so, why do you think those ramps

are there?

_____

_____

_____

Answer Key

Page 7
1. Is today your birthday?
2. A party is a wonderful idea.
3. Mike will bring the birthday cake.
4. How many candles will be on the cake?
5. Will there be a clown?
6. We can help you decorate.
7. Karen will bring the balloons.
8. The party will have lots of music.
9. There will be many presents.
10. What a wonderful birthday party it will be!

Page 8
Sentences:
2, 3, 5, 7, 8, 9, 10
Not sentences:
1, 4, 6

Page 9
Answers will vary.

Page 10
Answers will vary.

Page 11
1. Go to the office.
2. I've got to go see the principal!
3. I'm in big trouble!
4. Shut the door.
5. Tell me what you did.
6. I can't believe you put gum on the teacher's chair!
7. Bring your books and come with me.
8. Tell the teacher you are sorry.

Page 12
1. I like playing in the snow.
2. C
3. C
4. C
5. Hot chocolate tastes good on a cold day.
6. Do you want to ride my sled?
7. The snow will melt when the sun comes out.
8. How beautiful the snow is!
9. C
10. C

Page 13
Sentences:
1, 3, 4, 6, 7, 9
Not sentences:
2, 5, 8

Page 14
1. Cows and horses eat hay.
2. The ducks and geese swim.
3. Teachers and students read books.
4. Some of the pigs and the piglets sleep.
5. Sheep and goats graze.

Page 15
1. My family laughs at jokes and cries at sad movies.
2. The doctor met us at the hospital and told us where to wait.
3. Kayla caught and kept a bug.
4. The team won the game and was given a trophy.
5. We ate sandwiches and carrots.

Page 16
1. cat/kitten
2. teacher
3. present/gift
4. friends

Page 17
1. students
2. zoo
3. animals
4. monkeys
5. elephants
6. elephant
7. man
8. giraffe
9. we
10. Answers will vary.

Answer Key (cont.)

Page 18

1. standing
2. is
3. splash
4. wears
5. slides

Page 19

Predicates:

2., 3., 7., 9., 12., 13., 15., 18., 19.

Page 20

1. S
2. S
3. P
4. P
5. P
6. S
7. S
8. P
9. P
10. S

Page 21

Color:
rabbits hop
chefs cook
phones ring
glass breaks
ice melts
bug flies

Page 22

Person Nouns (Red):
brother
child
nurse
sister
teacher
Place Nouns (Yellow):
circus
hospital
school
store
bedroom
Thing Nouns (Blue):
book
car
crayons
desk
rainbow

Page 23

Answers will vary.

Page 24

Answers will vary.

Page 25

1. Saturday
2. More Candy
3. Rapone
4. Jack
5. Elm Street
6. Chocolicious
7. Mr.
8. Carole, Rhonda
9. Valentine's Day
10. Jack's

Page 26

Answers will vary.

Answer Key (cont.)

Page 27
1. P
2. P
3. S
4. P
5. P
6. P
7. P
8. S
9. P
10. S
11. S
12. P
13. P
14. S
15. P
16. S
17. S
18. P
19. S
20. P

Page 28
pigs
boxes
boys
foxes
dishes
taxes
churches
classes
rabbits
hats
wishes
passes

Page 29
1. b
2. b
3. a
4. b
5. b
6. b
7. a
8. a
9. a
10. b

Page 30
1. birds
2. families
3. porches
4. dinosaurs
5. mothers
6. daddies
7. glasses
8. foxes
9. cities
10. hangers

Page 31
1. I
2. We
3. they
4. she
5. her

Page 32
Answers will vary.
Subject pronouns:
1, 3, 5, 7

Page 33
1. his
2. Its
3. Her
4. my
5. mine
6.–10. Answers will vary.

Page 34
Answers will vary.

Answer Key (cont.)

Page 35
1. An
2. a
3. a
4. the
5. the
6. a
7. An
8. The
9. an
10. A

Page 36
Adjectives will vary.
1 (est)
2. (er)
3. (er)
4. (er)
5. (er)
6. (er)
7. (est)
8. (est)
9. (er)
10. (est)

Page 37
Action Verbs:
jump
eat
smile
stand
sit
Secret Code:
"V is for verb."

Page 38
1. baked
2. sang
3. opened
4. played
5. lost
6. won
7. ate
8. hurt
9. jumped
10. clapped

Page 39
1. crawls
2. eats
3. sits
4. meets
5. walks
6. ate
7. wont
8. dug
9. shopped
10. started

Page 40
1. b
2. d
3. c
4. f
5. g
6. e
7. a
8. h
9.–10. Answers will vary.

Page 41
Answers will vary.

Page 42
Possible combinations:
She is funny.
Kara is funny.
Derek is funny.
They are moving.
Frogs are moving.
Kara is pretty.
She is pretty.
Derek is eating.
She is eating.
Kara is eating.
Frogs are green.
They are green.

Page 43
Action Verbs:
wanted
bought
named
bit
love
needs
like
Linking Verbs:
is
is
is

Page 44
Answers will vary.

Answer Key *(cont.)*

Page 45
1. j
2. e
3. b
4. i
5. d
6. c
7. f
8. a
9. h
10. g

Page 46
1. isn't
2. aren't
3. wasn't
4. weren't
5. hasn't
6. haven't

Page 47
1. she's
2. we're
3. they're
4. we'll
5. it's
6. you're
7. I'm
8. she'll
9. they'll
10. he'd

Page 48
Answers will vary.

Page 49
Answers will vary.

Page 50
1. January, February, and March are usually cold months.
2. I like ballet, jazz, and tap.
3. My teachers are Mrs. Winters, Mr. Graves, Mrs. Willis, and Miss Scott.
4. He rode a train, a plane, and a car.
5. My favorite animals are dogs, cats, and rabbits.
6. Mercury, Venus, and Mars are all near the Earth.
7. Alicia, Dewanna, and Olivia all forgot their money.
8. Her favorite sports are softball, basketball, and soccer.
9. She had a penny, a nickel, and a dime.
10. The girl will wash, dry, and curl her hair.

Page 51
1.–6. Answers will vary.
7. January 6, 1930
8. March 3, 1997
9. September 12, 2006
10. April 20, 1967
11. July 4, 1776
12. August 10, 1973

Page 52
1. The plane landed in Atlanta, Georgia.
2. Each spring my grandmother visits Park City, Utah.
3. My pen pal lives in Decatur, Alabama.
4. Movies are made in Hollywood, California.
5.–8. Answers will vary.

Page 53
Answers will vary.

Page 54
1. Dear Karen,
2. Dear Aunt Sheryl,
3. Dear Curt,
4. Dear Coach Carter,
5. Love you,
6. Sincerely,
7. Yours truly,

Answer Key (cont.)

Page 55

1. d
2. c
3. f
4. b
5. a
6. e
7. I live at 321 Powder Mill Dr. in Oak City.
8. At the hospital, I met Dr. Richards.
9. Ms. Rose is my teacher.
10. Mr. and Mrs. Boyte will attend the party.

Page 56

Answers will vary.

Page 57

1. Makayla said, "You are very nice."
2. "I enjoy reading books," Jason said.
3. C
4. Samantha said, "We're going to be late."
5. The dentist asked, "Do you brush your teeth?"
6. C
7. C
8. Courtney said, "Spinach is delicious."

Page 58

Answers will vary.

Page 59

1. friendly
2. funny
3. upset
4. impolite
5. sorry
6. silent

Page 60

Answers will vary.

Page 61

1. friends
2. harder
3. walk
4. straight
5. homework

Page 62

1. get up
2. eat breakfast
3. go to work
4. eat lunch
5. go home
6. eat supper
7. get ready for bed
8. go to bed

Page 63

4—Jane got her birthday wish.
1—Jane wanted a puppy.
2—Jane's parents said she could not have a puppy.
3—Jane's birthday party finally arrived.

Page 64

Today my grandma took me to the pet store.
At the pet store, Grandma said I could get a pet.
I picked out a lizard.
I named him Spikey.
After she paid for the lizard, I could not wait to get Spikey home.
We definitely had a wonderful day at the pet store.

Page 65

First—He put toothpaste on the toothbrush.
Finally—He rinsed out the toothpaste.
Next—He brushed his teeth.
Finally—She tied her shoes.
First—She put her socks on her feet.
Next—She put her shoes on her feet.
Finally—You put the pieces of bread together.
Next—You put the peanut butter and jelly on the bread.
First—You get out the bread, the peanut butter, and the jelly.

Page 66

1. 1 3 2
2. 2 3 1

Answer Key *(cont.)*

Page 67

dark cloud with rain—umbrella

hurt finger—bandage

bright sun—sunglasses

patch of dirt being watered—flower growing

bunch of kittens—sign with kittens for sale

Page 68

Answers will vary.

Page 69

Answers will vary.

Page 70

1. O
2. O
3. F
4. F
5. O
6. F
7. O
8. F
9. O
10. F

Page 71

Answers will vary.

Page 72

Answers will vary.

Page 73

Answers may be as follows:

1. They do not look alike. They do not always act the same. Velvet likes to be outside; Vonda likes to be inside. Velvet likes to ride horses; Vonda likes to read. Velvet wants to be a veterinarian; Vonda wants to be a librarian.
2. They are twins. They have the same birthday. They each have a sister.

Page 74

True:

2, 5, 8, 9

Page 75

1. c
2. a
3. b
4. d

Page 76

Fantasy: 1b, 2a, 3b, 4b, 5a, 6a, 7a, 8a

Real: 1a, 2b, 3a, 4a, 5b, 6b, 7b, 8b

Page 77

Answers will vary.

Page 78

1. b
2. a

Page 79

Answers will vary.

Page 80

Answers will vary.

Page 81

1. Answers will vary.
   b. Going to the zoo was fun.
2. Answers will vary.
   a. One day we found a snake in the kitchen sink.

Page 82

A.

2—His name is Rufus.

1—My dog is a great pet.

4—After we play, I pet him and tell him he's the greatest dog in the world!

3—When Rufus and I play catch, he never misses the ball.

B.

4—Then my new tree house was finally ready!

2—First, my daddy said we had to get all of the supplies.

1—My daddy built me a tree house.

3—Next, we had to get busy working.

Answer Key *(cont.)*

Page 83

List A

cake

candy

caramel

chocolate

cookies

List B

panther

parrot

pelican

penguin

puppy

List C

Alex

Alicia

Allison

Amanda

Ann

Page 84

1. classes
2. buses
3. leaning
4. keeping
5. doing
6. greeted
7. brushes
8. heated
9. singing
10. shouting

Page 85

1. cupcake
2. snowman
3. suitcase
4. snowflake
5. hotdog
6.–8. Answers will vary.

Page 86

1. $3 + 5 = 8$
2. $8 + 2 = 10$
3. $16 + 1 = 17$
4. $10 + 4 = 14$
5. $11 + 3 = 14$

Page 87

1. 15
2. 14
3. 9
4. 6
5. 13
6. 14
7. 17
8. 6
9. 16
10. 15
11. 11
12. 9
13. 3
14. 2
15. 4
16. $2 + 5 = 7$

Page 88

1. 12	7. 7
2. 12	8. 15
3. 9	9. 18
4. 12	10. 18
5. 13	11. 13
6. 14	12. 10

Page 89

	Tens	Ones
1.	1	6
2.	1	1
3.	1	1
4.	1	4
5.	1	2

6. 1,7
7. 1,2
8. 1,4

Answer Key (cont.)

Page 90

1. 10
2. 14
3. 18
4. 4
5. 12
6. 6
7. 2
8. 8
9. 16
10. 5 + 5 = 10

Page 91

Blue equations:

1, 3, 4, 5, 6, 9

Yellow equations:

2, 7, 8

1. 6
2. 11
3. 4
4. 16
5. 14
6. 18
7. 3
8. 13
9. 8

Page 92

1. 20
2. 23
3. 16
4. 22
5. 20
6. 19
7. 17
8. 22
9. 20
10. 17

Page 93

1. 42
2. 76
3. 39
4. 34
5. 61
6. 28
7. 30
8. 90
9. 90
10. 43
11. 47
12. 83
13. 43
14. 23

Page 94

1. 996
2. 337
3. 234
4. 974
5. 796
6. 203
7. 877
8. 982
9. 1,000
10. 456
11. 914
12. 940
13.–15. Answers will vary.

Page 95

1. 576
2. 819
3. 889
4. 944
5. 983
6. 814
7. 552
8. 999
9. 666
10. 123 + 112 = 235
11. 312 + 200 = 512
12. 112 + 100 = 212

Answer Key *(cont.)*

Page 96

1. 11
2. 14
3. 8
4. 17
5. 30
6. 5
7. 10
8. 28

Secret Message:
YOU ARE COOL

Page 97

1. 108
2. 178
3. 522
4. 108
5. 588
6. 70
7. 82
8. 37
9. 180
10. 399
11. 99
12. 178
13. 453
14. 473
15. 389
16. 222

Page 98

1. 10, 7
2. 14, 6
3. 12, 6
4. 11, 4
5. 17, 9
6. 3, 1

Page 99

1. 5
2. 3
3. 3
4. 10
5. 8
6. 2
7. 5
8. 9
9. 7
10. 9
11. 0
12. 6
13. 9
14. 4
15. 5
16. 18
17. 5 - 4 = 1

Page 100

1. 16
2. 1
3. 16
4. 3
5. 1
6. 9
7. 2
8. 6
9. 9
10. 3
11. 7
12. 7

Page 101

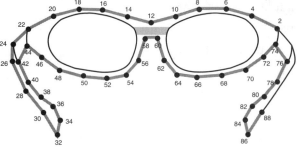

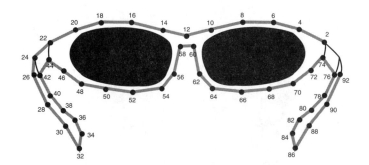

Answer Key *(cont.)*

Page 102

1. 6
2. 12
3. 18
4. 15
5. 9
6. 6, 12
7. 12, 18

Page 102 (cont.)

8. 12, 18, 24

Page 103

#1, #3, and #4 can all be counted by 5's.

5. 10, 25, 35, 45
6. 45, 55, 65, 70
7. 10, 20, 25, 30, 35, 40

15 items

Page 104

1. B
2. A
3. A
4. B
5. A

Page 105

10 ants
10 apples
10 ladybugs
10 rays on the sun
10 flowers

Page 106

1. 3 tens   1 one   31
2. 4 tens   6 ones   46
3. 1 ten   1 one   11
4. 5 tens   5 ones   55
5. 2 tens   3 ones   23

Page 107

1. 40
2. 80
3. 50
4. 100
5. 20, 50, 70
6. 40, 70, 90
7. 50, 70, 90
8. 10 + 20 + 10 = 40

Page 108

1. 42   7. 65, 55
2. 50, 40   8. 87, 67
3. 42   9. 10
4. 81, 61   10. 10
5. 65   11. 10
6. 33, 13   12. 10

Page 109

Circles:

1, 5, 7, 9

X's:

2, 3, 4, 6, 8, 10

11.–12. Answers will vary.

Page 110

Answers will vary.

Page 111

1. 30
2. 10
3. 30
4. 50
5. 10
6. Answers will vary.

Page 112

1. 7 > 3
2. 6 > 2
3. 1 < 5
4. 9 > 3
5. 3 < 4

Answer Key (cont.)

Page 113
1. L G
   23 < 32
2. L G
   18 < 81
3. G L
   45 > 12
4. L G
   30 < 40
5. L G
   10 < 100
6. L G
   26 < 27
7. G L
   76 > 62
8. G L
   17 > 11
9.–10. Answers will vary.

Page 114
1. 7
2. 58
3. 13
4. 34
Blue:
1–14
Yellow:
16–30

Page 115
1. Crede: 4th
2. Dan: 8th
3. Sandy: 7th
4. Riley: 5th
5. Mike: 6th

Page 116
1. 5th grade
2. 1st grade
3. 3rd grade
4. 4th grade

Page 117
Color every 1st picture green.
Color every 3rd picture purple.
Color every 5th picture red.

Page 118
1. 1 + 5 + 25 = 31 cents
2. 25 + 25 + 10 = 60 cents
3. 20 + 4 = 24 cents
4. 10 + 5 + 1 = 16 cents
5. 50 + 30 = 80 cents
6. 65 cents
7. 55 cents

Page 119

Page 120
1. 24 cents
2. 55 cents
3. 75 cents
4. 2 quarters
5. 67 cents, 6 dimes, 1 nickel, 2 pennies

Page 121
1. 70 cents
2. 72 cents
3. 56 cents
4. 100 cents
5. 50 cents
Thinking about Money:
Answers will vary.

Page 122
1. 1:30
2. 12:00
3. 5:00
4. 3:30
8:30 is closest to the time you go to bed.

Page 123
1. 2:30
2. 7:00
3. 12:00
4. 11:30

Answer Key *(cont.)*

Page 124

1. 7:15
2. 12:35
3. 2:05
4. 6:50
5. 4:20
6. 10:45

Page 125

Answers will vary.

Page 126

1. 9:30
2. 9:30
3. The Animal Show starts first.
   It starts at 10:00.
4. 5 hours
5. 13 1/2 hours

Page 127

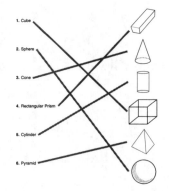

Page 128

1. 7
2. 12
3. 4
4. January
5. Answers will vary.
6. March
7. August
8. February

Page 129

1. 2 hours
2. Answers will vary.
3. 9:00
4. 7 days
5. 61 days
6. 2 hours

Page 130

1. IIII IIII
2. IIII IIII
3. IIII III
4. III
5. Answers will vary.
6. IIII II

Page 131

1. Hawaii
2. Texas
3. Florida and Texas
4. Answers will vary.

Page 132

Page 133

1. cone
2. rectangular prism
3. cone
4. sphere
5. cube
6. pyramid
7. cylinder
8. cube
9. sphere

Page 134

Color all the rectangles blue.
Color all the squares red.
Color all the triangles green.
Color all the circles yellow.

Page 135

Answers will vary.

Page 136

Line of symmetry:
Square, ice-cream cone, four-leaf clover, letter H,
T-shirt, triangle, star, button

5. Answers will vary.

Answer Key (cont.)

Page 137

1. 6 inches
2. 4 inches
3. 5 inches
4. 3 inches

Page 138

Color the 3-inch fries yellow.
Color the 4-inch fries green.
Color the 5-inch fries red.
Color the leftover fries blue.

Page 139

1. 4 cm
2. 1 cm
3. 5 cm
4. 2 cm
5. 7 cm
6. 9 cm

Page 140

Answers will vary.

Page 141

Yellow:
necklace
tube of lipstick
feather
penny
dollar bill
Green:
car
tree
horse
guitar
dog

Page 142

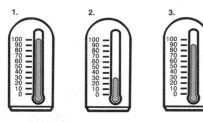

Page 143

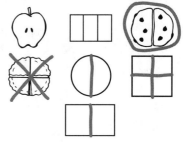

Page 144

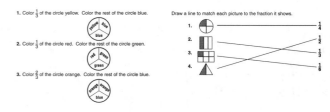

Page 145

Page 146

These numbers should be circled:
1, 7, 23, 28, 36, 63, 64, 70, 100, 150, 200, 278, 295, 300, 301, 343, 384, 392, 400, 420, 438, 483, 490, 497, 500

Page 147

1. 861
2. 999
3. 742
4. 815
5. 467
6. 623

Think About It:
$9.00

Page 148

1. 984
2. 863
3. 731
4. 831

Answer Key (cont.)

Page 149

1. before
2. between
3. between
4. after

Page 150

1. 459	876	951
2. 697	796	976
3. 455	456	457
4. 400	600	900
5. 152	215	512

Think About It:

1. 3, 11, 40
2. 100, 400, 450

Page 151

Correct problems:

2, 3, 5, 8, 9, 10

How many zeros did you find? 6

Page 152

1. 1	6. 1
2. 8	7. 1
3. 1	8. 2
4. 4	9. 11
5. 3	

Page 153

1. 2	7. 14
2. 4	8. 16
3. 6	9. 18
4. 8	10. 20
5. 10	11. 22
6. 12	12 24

Page 154

4x3=11	4x3=12	3x1=3	3x9=27	3x8=29	3x2=9
3x1=0	3x4=9	3x2=0	3x1=3	3x11=11	3x12=33
2x3=18	3x8=24	3x12=36	7x3=21	6x3=12	3x1=4
9x3=17	3X0=3	2X3=8	3X9=27	3X10=40	7X3=29
3X3=11	3X6=18	3X2=6	7X3=21	3X6=36	3X1=6
3X0=30	5X3=14	3X7=24	9X3=17	3X4=7	6X3=9

Page 155

1. 0	28	4	48
2. 44	12	32	24
3. 8	20	36	40
4. 4	32	8	28

Page 156

1. 25
2. 35
3. 5
4. 10
5. 40

$10 \times 10 = 100$

Page 157

1. $2 \times 1 = 2$
2. $3 \times 3 = 9$
3. $5 \times 8 = 40$
4. $4 \times 4 = 16$

Page 158

1. 6	6
2. 20	20
3. 18	18
4. 32	32

Page 159

11, 21, 0, 16, 48, 25, 60

Page 160

These numbers should be circled:

1, 2, 4, 5

6. B
7. C
8. A
9. D

Page 161

Answers will vary.

Page 162

1. 50
2. states
3. 13
4. Betsy Ross
5. States, America

Answer Key (cont.)

Page 163
1. 5
2. 7
3. Answers will vary.
4. A pizza party
5. The pizza party received the most votes.

Page 164
1.–3. executive, legislative, judicial
4. President—leads our country
5. Congress—makes the laws for our country
6. Supreme Court—decides if the laws are fair
7. Government—has three branches

Just for Fun:
Answers will vary.

Page 165
Answers will vary.

Page 166
Answers will vary.

Page 167
The following boxes should have
an X on them: 1,3

Page 168
Answers will vary.

Page 169
Answers will vary.

Page 170
1. symbol
2. map key
3. compass rose
4. map title
5. location
6. directions

Page 171
Answers will vary.

Page 172
Answers will vary.

Page 173
Answers will vary.

Page 174
1. forest   4. mountain
2. desert   5. ocean
3. island

Page 175
1. ocean
2. desert
3. city
4. river
5. farm
6. neighborhood

Page 176

Page 177
1. globe   5. island
2. equator   6. conservation
3. resource   7. continents
4. oceans   8. geography

Mystery words:
Our Earth

Page 178
Seven continents:
North America
South America
Europe
Africa
Asia
Australia
Antarctica
Four Oceans:
Pacific Ocean
Atlantic Ocean
Arctic Ocean

Answer Key (cont.)

Indian Ocean

Page 179
1. present
2. past
3. present
4. past

Page 180
Answers will vary.

Page 181
Answers will vary.**Page 182**
4—Man landed on the moon.
1—Columbus discovered America.
2—George Washington became the first president of the United States.
3—Women were given the right to vote in the United States.
5—I was born.

Page 183
1. history—the story of the past
2. landmark—a well-known object at a certain place
3. settler—a person who makes his or her home in a new place
4. shelter—a place where people live
5. colony—a place ruled by another country

Page 184
Answers will vary.

Page 185
1. Rhonda
2. Rhonda
3. Shelly
4. Robert

Page 186
a. 0
b. 2
c. 3
d. 1
e. 4

Page 187
Answers will vary.

Page 188

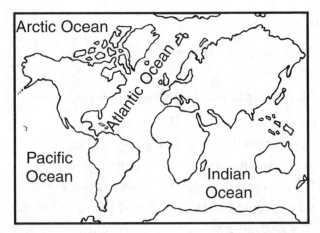

Page 189
Answers will vary.

Page 190
Answers will vary.

Page 191

Page 192
1. T
2. F
3. T
4. T
5. T
6. F

Page 193
3, 2, 5, 1, 6, 4

Page 194
Answers will vary.

Answer Key (cont.)

Page 195
1. flower
2. pollen
3. leaf
4. stem
5. seeds
6. roots

Page 196
1. tree—log house
2. tomato plant—bottle of ketchup
3. aloe plant—aloe—lotion
4. cotton plant—T-shirt

Page 197
Answers will vary.

Page 198
1. air
2. eggs
3. insects
4. Frogs
5. feathers
6. mammals

Page 199
1. 6
2. head, thorax, abdomen
3. head
4. spider
5. Answers will vary.

Page 200
Each answer should reflect its caption.

Page 201
1. puppy—dog
2. fawn—deer
3. calf—cow
4. colt—horse
5. kitten—cat
6. chick—chicken

Page 202
1. predator
2. prey
3. predator
4. prey
5. fish
6. Answers will vary.

Page 203
1. d
2. a
3. b
4. c
5. e

Page 204
1. sunny
2. Yes, they are expecting snow.
3. The people in California are having partly cloudy weather.
4. It is most likely to rain in the Midwest.

Page 205
1. Answers will vary.
2. Summer
1. Answers will vary.
2. Winter
1. Answers will vary.
2. Spring
1. Answers will vary.
2. Fall

Page 206
1. Sunday had the lowest temperature.
2. Saturday had the highest temperature.
3. Monday and Friday had the same temperature.
4. On Sunday it was cold enough for snow.
5. Wednesday's temperature was 40 degrees.

Page 207
1. evaporation
2. condensation
3. precipitation

Page 208
1. rain
2. sleet
3. rainbow
4. snow
5. storm
6. blizzard
7. tornado
8. hurricane

Answer Key *(cont.)*

Page 209
1. happy face
2. birthday cake
3. dog
4. snake

nimbus, stratus, cumulus, cirrus

Page 210
Answers will vary.

Page 211
1. Answers will vary.
2. Answers will vary.
3. Answers will vary.
4. endangered
5. Answers will vary.

Page 212
1. spins
2. the same direction
3. does not move
4. day or night
5. day
6. 24
7. 24
8. star

Page 213
Answers will vary.

Page 214
1. c
2. a
3. d
4. b

Page 215

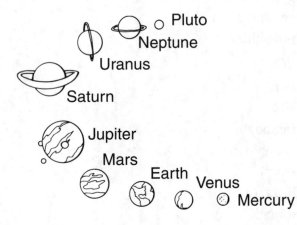

1.–2. Answers will vary.

Page 216
1. liquid
2. solid
3. gas
4. solid
5. Answers will vary.

Page 217

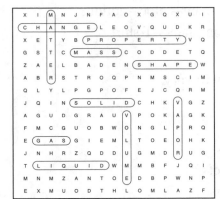

Page 218
Answers will vary.

Page 219
1. push
2. pull
3. pull
4. push

Page 220

Page 221
Answers will vary.